D1490370

Combating Hatred

Combating Hatred

Transformational Educators Striving for Social Justice

Second Edition

Terrance L. Furin

ROWMAN & LITTLEFIELD
Lanham • Boulder • New York • London

Published by Rowman & Littlefield
An imprint of The Rowman & Littlefield Publishing Group, Inc.
4501 Forbes Boulevard, Suite 200, Lanham, Maryland 20706
https://rowman.com

Unit A, Whitacre Mews, 26-34 Stannary Street, London SE11 4AB,
United Kingdom

British Library Cataloguing in Publication Information Available

Library of Congress Cataloging-in-Publication Data

Names: Furin, Terrance L., 1940- author.
Title: Combating hatred : transformational educators striving for social
 justice / Terrance L. Furin.
Description: Second Edition. | Lanham, Maryland : Rowman & Littlefield,
 [2018] | Includes bibliographical references.
Identifiers: LCCN 2018028869 (print) | LCCN 2018029087 (ebook) | ISBN
 9781475842968 | ISBN 9781475842944 (Cloth : alk. paper) | ISBN
 9781475842951 (Paperback : alk. paper)
Subjects: LCSH: School violence--United States--Case studies. | Hate--United
 States. | Educational leadership--United States.
Classification: LCC LB3013.3 (ebook) | LCC LB3013.3 .F87 2018 (print) | DDC
 371.7/82--dc23
LC record available at https://lccn.loc.gov/2018028869

♾ ™ The paper used in this publication meets the minimum requirements of American
National Standard for Information Sciences Permanence of Paper for Printed Library
Materials, ANSI/NISO Z39.48-1992.

Printed in the United States of America

For my wife Mary Ann, who has given Varykyno and so much more.

For my children, Kathleen, Jennifer, Timothy, and Molly,
who are my best teachers.

For my grandchildren,
Jasmine, Aya, Timothy, Chaundra, Saoirse, Santana, and Emiliano.

May they know a world without hatred.

Contents

List of Figures

Preface

Combating Hatred: Transformational Educators Striving for Social Justice grew from an earlier book titled *Combating Hatred: Educators Leading the Way* (2009). The genesis for a new book was the September 22, 2013, headline in a relatively small local newspaper that read "CASD in Crisis after Racially-Charged Text Messages Surfaced." This article described a dramatic series of texts between the district's superintendent and athletic director that contained startling examples of raw racism at its worst—this in a district in which a majority of students were black or Hispanic.

I was deeply troubled by this incident because I had been a superintendent for twenty-two years and I hold that position in high esteem. It pained me to see it sullied in such a way. I struggled for more than two years to try and find ways to analyze and explain adequately this episode for my doctoral students at Saint Joseph's University in Philadelphia, where I teach prospective school leaders in our doctoral program. It was not until after several failed attempts at an article that I contacted Jay Goldman, the editor of *School Administrator*, the national publication of the American Association of School Administrators (AASA). This monthly publication reaches more than fifteen thousand school leaders nationally, and my hope was that what I had written might be published so that other school leaders could learn from this incident and become transformational leaders in their own way.

After many revisions with the editors from AASA, an article titled "Combating Hatred among Us" was published in the November 2017 edition of *School Administrator*. I have used it with several groups of superintendents and doctoral students to draw attention to the need for true transformational educators to become leaders for social justice and equity. This book's first chapter begins with a description and analysis of this racist text crisis. Even though there is material in the remaining six chapters from the earlier book, significant portions are new and reflective of the many challenges facing school leaders today.

Much has changed since *Combating Hatred: Educators Leading the Way* was published in 2009. Much has also remained the same. Hatred among us has actually gotten worse with the continued presence, and perhaps growth, of hate groups. Open prejudice and racism from neo-Nazi, Aryan Nation, skinheads, and other groups present very daunting challenges for school leaders. The raw racism these groups exemplify by their existence and by their overt actions present not only challenges but also opportunities for school leaders to become transformational.

To be successful in doing this, these leaders need to recognize the importance of placing students and teachers at the center of educational experiences. Without knowing the theory, when I began teaching I tried to build all educational activities around the experiences and needs of my students. Later I learned that this is the progressive philosophy of John Dewey. I modeled his philosophy as a teacher for twelve years in junior and senior high school. It also formed the basis of my leadership style as an assistant superintendent for five years and a superintendent for twenty-two.

Luckily I had outstanding principals and other mentors who believed in democracy not only in their leadership styles but more importantly as the essence of our society. Such leadership resonated with me because of my strong belief in the democratic principles upon which our nation was founded. This is understandable considering that I was a former social studies teacher with a master's degree in history and a PhD in American studies.

There are many case studies and role models in this book. I know all of them, and they have been inspirations for my life's mission. The final chapter in the book presents five educators who I believe are truly transformational. They were selected because they met criteria for leaders who dedicated their lives in being change agents in trying to achieve social justice for all Americans.

I am grateful to several Jesuits and my colleagues at Saint Joseph's University as well as several former and current school leaders for being inspirations in my life. I am also thankful for my children (Kathy, Jenny, Tim, and Molly), from whom I learned more than I ever taught. To me they are, to use a Jesuit term, "women and men for others." Most of all I am indebted to my wife, Mary Ann, who has lived through each of the case studies in the book with me. She is my number one mentor and editor. Her life is deeply imbued with a general love for all of humanity. As a preschool teacher (which translates to many, many hours of hard work and very little pay), she strives daily to create a world in which hatred is lessened and love for all can be not just a dream but a reality.

TLF

Acknowledgments

Acknowledgment needs to be given to the editors of publications for granting permission to reprint portions of material that appeared elsewhere. Reprinted with permission from *School Administrator* magazine, published by the School Superintendents Association, the following: the February 2004 issue of *School Administrator* for "Tragedy at the Top" by Terrance L. Furin; the November 2007 issue of *School Administrator* for "Confronting a Neo-Nazi Hate Group" by Terrance Furin; and the November 2017 issue of *School Administrator* for "Combating Hatred among Us" by Terrance L. Furin. An earlier version of the "Motorhead Club" contained in chapter 4 appeared in an article titled "Cult of Self: Arrogance and the Death of History" that appeared in *Culture Clash/Media Demons*, copyright 2004, by Chelsea House Publishers, an imprint of Infobase Learning.

I wish to acknowledge the many wonderful professional educators who gave of their time to read portions of the manuscript before it became a book. Special thanks go to my colleagues at Saint Joseph's University: Drs. Aimee La Pointe Terosky, Encarnacion Rodriguez, Owen Gilman, and Fr. Dan Joyce. Thanks also go to the individuals who are presented as case studies in this book as they have read the sections that concern them. They are Frank Murphy, Ellen Keys, Marty Kane, Tom Asad, David Jarvie, Sister Rosemary Hocevar, Jack Thomas, and Lucille Lang, the wife of Leonard Lang, who is deceased. Special thanks go to my wife, Mary Ann, who is a voracious reader and a student of the English language. She has provided invaluable insight on an ongoing basis.

Acknowledgments are also given to the professionalism of my editors at Rowman & Littlefield, Tom Koerner, Christopher Fischer, and Carlie Wall, who have treated me with the utmost respect and provided valuable editing and publishing suggestions. Without them, especially Tom Koerner, this book would never have been written.

Introduction

Combating Hatred: Transformational Educators Striving for Social Justice

All should just have whatever first names they want . . . then last name is N----
R! Leroy N----r, Preacher N----r, Night train n----r, Clarence n----r, Latoya n---
-r, Thelma n----r and so on. [1]

This quotation is taken from a series of text messages, sent on school district phones, between a school superintendent and an athletic director in an urban/ suburban school district outside Philadelphia. This hate-filled act represents an underlying prejudice that became exposed when a local newspaper reported the texts. It is only one example of hatred that has become increasingly present in the fabric of American life, where the recognized number of hate groups has nearly doubled between 1999 and 2016. [2]

These hate groups are found in nearly every state. For example, in 2017 the Southern Poverty Law Center (SPLC) listed Alabama as having twenty-seven hate groups, while Pennsylvania had forty. [3] The SPLC defines a hate group "as an organization that—based on its official statements or principles, the statements of its leaders, or its activities—has beliefs or practices that attack or malign an entire class of people, typically for their immutable characteristics." [4]

This book is about hatred that is oftentimes manifested in actions that have impacted education in various ways. It is also about educators who became transformational leaders to combat hatred and strive for social justice. Rather than trying to quantify hatred, several vignettes depicting actual experiences are presented. These include:

- raw racist texts exchanged between an urban/suburban school superintendent and the district's athletic director that expose deep-seated hatred that led to a school community being ripped apart (chapter 1);
- neo-Nazi attempts to recruit new Aryan members and disrupt education by distributing flyers calling for a boycott of schools in a rural/suburban school district on the anniversary of Heinrich Himmler's death (chapter 2);
- violent school shootings and an examination of educational philosophies and resulting school curricula and structures that may help explain one of the major causes of student alienation and consequent hatred (chapter 3);
- hanging nooses as symbols of racial hatred that appeared in a rural high school in Louisiana in 2006 and an urban/suburban high school in Pennsylvania in 2017 (chapter 4); and
- religious intolerance when hatred manifested over school prayer tore a school district and community apart (chapter 5).

Each of the first five chapters contains not only descriptions of hatred but also numerous true-life examples of educators who in one way or another can be considered transformational because of their striving to achieve a more complete sense of social justice for their students and communities.

Chapter 6 is solely about five transformational leaders whose commitment to social justice values is inspirational. They are:

- a curriculum coordinator in Cleveland's largest suburb who transformed a traditional, chronological, facts-driven junior and senior high school social studies curriculum into a dynamic course of studies that addressed serious social justice issues threatening the very survival of our human species;
- a principal of a Catholic women's high school who led the designing of a new high school based on the school's mission, which resulted in a groundbreaking new building containing an innovative student-centered curriculum that emphasized social justice ideals;
- a suburban school superintendent whose democratic vision for students to have suitable facilities and a meaningful curriculum united a badly divided community by providing funding for a distressed school district;
- a Jesuit saint whose sense of social justice included developing a public pedagogy that turned the entire nation of Chile into an educational model based on both traditional Catholic theological principles and the philosophy of John Dewey's child-centered progressivism; and
- an educator and arts advocate whose sense of social justice motivated her to develop mural arts projects for Philadelphia that have made it the mural arts capital of the world.

METHODS OF PRESENTATION

In addition to a traditional style of writing, this book uses two methods that are considered less traditional. One is an interdisciplinary method that breaks down barriers often found in traditional disciplines so as to provide richer contexts and help readers become fluid in their thinking about the material being considered. The second less traditional method is a scholar-practitioner approach that helps unite theory and practice so that educational leaders can be grounded in theory while facing practical issues.

Interdisciplinary Methodology

Interdisciplinary thinking and processing can break down the barricades that exist between disciplines and cause creativity that goes beyond limitations often imposed by separate disciplines' strict methodologies. Thomas Kuhn's *The Structure of Scientific Revolutions*[5] lays the groundwork for interdisciplinary thinking. Kuhn describes ways that rigid paradigms become flexible because of anomalies that in turn lead to the collapse of the old paradigms and the emergence of new ones. This he labels a scientific revolution.

One of Kuhn's examples of a scientific revolution occurred when Ptolemy's view of our solar system depicting the earth at the center collapsed and was replaced by Copernicus's theory that the sun was the center. The old paradigm went through a paradigm shift and was eventually replaced by a new one. Interdisciplinary methodologies often are the catalysts that help cause paradigm shifts and therefore broaden our perspectives. By expanding our thinking, they show different possibilities and cause us to see and create new paradigms.

A good example of this process is seen in the field of history. Stanley Elkins's book *Slavery*[6] is a classic interdisciplinary study of American slavery. In this book Elkins compares aspects of American slavery with the Nazi Holocaust. He weaves together history, sociology, economics, and psychology in a manner that sheds a different light on American slavery. His doctoral dissertation at the University of Chicago formed the basis for the book and was initially rejected by members of his committee from the History Department because his study and analyses moved outside of traditional history methodology. He eventually received his PhD, and the book is now considered a classic in American studies that uses a highly interdisciplinary approach for both research and practical applications.

Interdisciplinary methods often use aesthetic experiences found in literature, music, and art to make connections that help enrich various topics. Maxine Greene, a disciple of John Dewey, described the effects that aesthetic experiences can have on individuals when she wrote, "We experience a sense of surprise oftentimes, an acute sense that things may look otherwise, feel otherwise, *be* otherwise than we have assumed—and suddenly the world seems new, with possibilities still to be explored."[7]

A good example of Greene's interdisciplinary connections is her use of American literature to make a rich association with the foundations of our democracy. This happens in her consideration of Mark Twain's *Adventures of Huckleberry Finn*. After presenting portions of the novel she focuses on the critical scene in which the steamboat crashes into Huck and Jim's raft, ending their idyllic journey down the Mississippi River. Technology smashes their pastoral world. Greene makes connections this way:

> There is no fatality in the steamboat "pounding along," not if we try to "see her good" and pose our questions and try seriously to understand. Individuals can still link hands and enact democracy. They can still establish their own dominion and supremacy by rejecting the givenness of the mechanical and the impersonal. Working together, reflecting together, forging community together, they may at last surpass what is intolerable; they may yet transform their world.[8]

Rather than viewing the pastoral/ technological dialectic as something negative, she proposes that by "working together, reflecting together, forging community together, they may at last surpass what is intolerable; they may yet transform their world."

Disciplines other than aesthetic ones also can be used to create rich contexts for deeper understandings. These include philosophy, political science, psychology, and history. The field of education is a natural one to incorporate these along with aesthetics into an interdisciplinary approach. Educators already freely use the terms "paradigm" and "paradigm shift" in their vocabularies. If we educators are willing to move beyond traditional areas of study that emphasize practical applications such as testing, finance, strategic planning, human resource supervision, curriculum implementation, and organization management, then new worlds of unlimited possibilities can open to us.

This is the main reason that an interdisciplinary methodology is used throughout this book. It can help provide a rich context for the examination of hatred and transformational educators' responses to it. Some examples found in the text that stretch us beyond those usually addressed in the traditional field of education are as follows:

- Literature: Ernest Hemingway's *The Old Man and the Sea*, Toni Morrison's *The Bluest Eye*, William Faulkner's *The Sound and the Fury*
- Music: Henryk Górecki's *Symphony No. 3*, Simon and Garfunkel's *The Sound of Silence*
- Art: Mural Arts Philadelphia, Charlie Chaplin's *Modern Times*
- Philosophy: John Locke's *An Essay Concerning Human Understanding*, Jean Jacques Rousseau's *On the Social Contract* and *Emile, or On Education*, Michel Foucault's *Discipline and Punish*

- Political science: James MacGregor Burns's *Leadership* and *Transforming Leadership*
- Psychology: George Kelly's *A Theory of Personality*
- History: David Wallace Adams's *Education for Extinction*

While interdisciplinary methodology can help provide a rich context for the examination of hatred and transformational leaders' responses to it, a scholar-practitioner approach provides the substantial foundation for that examination.

Scholar/Practitioner

The importance of school leaders being scholar-practitioners cannot be over-emphasized. Practitioners who act without theoretical roots often become reactionaries who drift wherever the latest educational fad, political wind, or pressure group pushes them. On the other hand, scholars who develop theories on isolated campuses oftentimes do not see those theories blossom into fruitful realities because of the isolation that exists between them and practitioners in the field.

An interesting approach in determining the extent of the scholar-practitioner gap has been described by Perry A. Zirkel, an education professor at Lehigh University. In his article "The Professoriate, the Practitioners, and 'Their' Periodicals," found in the April 2007 issue of *Kappan*, he reports on a survey conducted among university professors and school superintendents.

This survey asked each person to indicate the journal that they read most from a list of fifteen popular ones. What he found was that a huge breach existed between refereed journals read by professors and practitioner magazines read by superintendents. This can create enormous problems for those interested in being effective school leaders as they usually fall on one side or the other and seldom enter the space between.

The two most popular journals read by professors were *Educational Administration Quarterly* and *American Educational Research Journal*. Superintendents' choices were *The School Administrator* and *The American School Board Journal*. Zirkel recognized the seriousness of this situation and wrote that "each group must continually inform the other if educational leadership is to be effective."[9] Effective leaders are those who bridge this gap and enter the space between the two extremes.

Two educational theorists, Patrick Jenlink of Stephen Austin State University and Raymond Horn, formerly of Saint Joseph's University, recognized the need to bridge this gap when they started a new journal, *Scholar-Practitioner Quarterly*, in 2002 to provide a forum for scholar-practitioner discourse. They believed that "the future of education rests, in large part, on the fostering of new perspectives for leadership of our educational institutions."[10]

The scholar-practitioner approach hopefully will provide new perspectives for educational leaders. Throughout this book practical examples are given to illuminate educational theories. These should help make abstract ideas come to life. Theories are presented in a straightforward way so that practitioners can form a philosophic foundation that grounds their actions.

This book is about hatred and about transformational educators whose strong sense of social justice leads them to combat hatred. Let us begin with chapter 1, which describes an ugly exchange of raw racist texts between a school superintendent and the district's athletic director. After presenting this situation, the chapter focuses on ways that individual educational leaders can look inward and assess their core values, enabling them to become transformational leaders of others through similar reflections.

NOTES

1. Michael Price and Kristina Scala, "CASD in Crisis after Racially-Charged Text Messages Surface," *Daily Local News*, September 22, 2013, 1 (note: the "n" word is spelled out in the original quotation).

2. "Hate Groups 1999–2016," Southern Poverty Law Center, https://www.splcenter.org/hate-map (accessed February 3, 2018).

3. Ibid.

4. "Frequently Asked Questions about Hate Groups," Southern Poverty Law Center, https://www.splcenter.org/20171004/frequently-asked-questions-about-hate-groups#hate%20group (accessed April 2, 2018).

5. Thomas Kuhn, *The Structure of Scientific Revolutions* (Chicago: University of Chicago Press, 1996).

6. Stanley Elkins, *Slavery* (Chicago: University of Chicago Press, 1968).

7. Maxine Greene, *Variations on a Blue Guitar* (New York: Teachers College Press), 116.

8. Maxine Greene, "Steamboats and Critiques," in *Landscapes of Learning* (New York: Teachers College Press, 1978), 124.

9. Perry Zirkel, "The Professoriate, the Practitioners, and 'Their' Periodicals," *Phi Delta Kappan* (April 2007): 588.

10. Patrick Jenlink and Raymond Horn, "Introducing the Scholar-Practitioner Quarterly," *Scholar-Practitioner Quarterly* 1, no. 1 (Fall 2002): 6.

Chapter One

Combating Hatred and Creating Leadership from Within

Leadership springs from *within*. It's about *who I am* as much as what I do.[1]

Leadership is not a job, not a role one plays at work and then puts aside during the commute home in order to relax and enjoy real life. Rather leadership is the leader's real life.[2]

LEADERSHIP THAT GROWS FROM WITHIN

Chris Lowney, in his book *Heroic Leadership*, provides some important insights that may help us understand the type of educational leadership crucial for success as we move further into the twenty-first century. The two quotations from Lowney's book *Heroic Leadership* that begin this chapter capture some of the essence that he believes have enabled the Jesuits, the largest Catholic religious order in the world, to not only survive but also flourish for more than 460 years.

Drawing on his former life as a Jesuit priest, Lowney presents four "pillars of success" that he considers important in explaining Jesuit endurance: "self-awareness, ingenuity, love, and heroism."[3] "Self-awareness" in particular is consistent with the opening quotation that "leadership springs from *within*." If we accept that true leadership, indeed leadership that can be transformational, is "about *who I am* as much as what I do," then the following shocking description of an incident that occurred at an urban/suburban school district outside of Philadelphia reveals an inner self hidden by an external mask.

A SCHOOL SUPERINTENDENT'S CRISIS

Raw Racism from a Supposedly Trusted Leader

The September 22, 2013, headline in the Sunday *Daily Local News* dramatically read "CASD in Crisis after Racially-Charged Text Messages Surface."[4] This news story featured the school superintendent, Richard Como, and the district's athletic director, James Donato. The account shook the southeastern Pennsylvania Coatesville school district with tremors that continue to this day. Here is a printable sampling of the texts (others are too obscene or just plain filthy to include):

June 4
Donato to Como:
"All should just have whatever first names they want . . . then last name is N----R! Leroy N----r, Preacher N----r, Night train n----r, Clarence n----r, La-toya n----r, Thelma n----r and so on."[5]
Como to Donato:
"Great idea! Joe n----r bill n----r snake n----r got a nice ring to it."
Donato to Como:
"LMAO!"[6]
Como to Donato:
"hahahahahahahhahahahahaha could have whole homerooms of N----r! haha-hahahahahaha! Will N----r report to office, pardon the interruption but will N----r report to nurses office. N----r to lunch now!"

June 7
Como to Donato (referring to pending teacher layoffs):
" . . . 23 get clipped Tuesday . . ."
Donato to Como:
"How many n----rs out of 23? Not enough!"
Como to Donato:
"Don't know but think it's only 4-5. At most until last minute rush of firing by Goo of Phoenix and Kamara."
Donato to Como:
"Good hangings there!"

The ongoing exchange containing sexually explicit remarks regarding interracial sex acts as well as offensive racial, ethnic, and sexual remarks against African Americans, Jews, Arabs, and women continued until June 17, 2013. The texts were especially dramatic considering the school's racially and ethnically diverse student body, which in 2014 consisted of 49.6 percent white, 36.1 percent black, 11.7 percent Hispanic, and 2.6 percent Asian, American Indian, Pacific Islander, or mixed.[7]

The texts came to light after the district's technology director, Abdallah Hawa (referred to in one of the texts as a "camel jockey"), was cleansing

Donato's district cell phone for reuse after it had been replaced at Donato's request because it was white and therefore too "girly." Deeply upset after he saw some of the texts, Hawa contacted a district administrator, who turned it over to a school board member.

The matter remained private until the September 22 *Daily Local News* story brought the matter to the public's attention. The publication resulted in more than one thousand irate individuals attending the school board meeting on September 25 at which the board had scheduled a vote to accept Como's and Donato's resignations. More than three hours of angry, blistering comments made clear that the public wanted the men fired and the entire school board to resign. Ultimately the board did accept the two resignations citing feared legal problems if Como and Donato were fired outright. [8]

Como and Donato immediately vanished from view. Como still possesses his Pennsylvania superintendent certificate, and both he and Donato are collecting their state pensions. Lawsuits regarding possible misuse of funds that were also mentioned in the texts were resolved when a jury found Como guilty of multiple counts of felony theft on January 26, 2018. Even though a new Coatesville superintendent has done much to calm the situation, anger still simmers below the surface more than five years after the texts were exposed.

The outcry and resentment expressed by employees, students, and the public were generally of disbelief followed by deep anger. Como had been someone who was admired by most students and residents in the district as he had been a winning high school football coach, assistant principal, and high school principal prior to becoming the superintendent in 2005. One former Coatesville student and past employee (who asked to remain anonymous) had been recommended for her position by Como. She was particularly distraught by the news of the text exchanges and wrote this about the incident:

> Mr. Como was my principal and was very kind to me. I've always had a dream of giving back to my school district and Mr. Como gave me an opportunity to do so. I can't help but wonder if I was just another "N" word to him? With tears in my eyes, as much as I would like to be exempt . . . I'm sure that I'm not. More importantly, this was the face for Coatesville's education? I am so upset and can only pray that God will bless my kids with Administrators [*sic*] and teachers that have their best interest at heart and are not just using them for athletic purposes. [9]

This feeling of betrayal was only one of many that were expressed by confused and exasperated citizens and students. Some but not all professional educators shared similar views.

Some School Leaders' Reactions to the Racial Texts

The texts formed the basis for dialogue in roundtable sessions at a 2016 Pennsylvania Association of School Administrators superintendents conference and the 2017 American Association of School Administrators national conference. The majority of views expressed were of shock or disbelief. Some, however, indicated that the texts should be viewed as little more than casual locker room banter or that the real wrongdoing was that the texts were sent on district-owned cell phones. One superintendent commented that had the texts been on private phones their appropriateness would not have been questioned.

Countering this was a comment made by an individual who teaches prospective superintendents at a university near the affected district. She said that a distinction should be made between a person's personality (defined as surface persona) and character (internally held core beliefs). Another superintendent from a district near a large Midwestern city commented that if personality and character are not in sync then the outer charade will eventually decay and reveal the internal self.[10] This can lead to individual moral collapse and jeopardize the integrity of the entire school district's professed values. This certainly seems to be the case of the now infamous superintendent and athletic director.

These later views should cause concern, and we should question whether the Coatesville superintendent is an anomaly or if there are other school leaders among the roughly fourteen thousand school districts in the United States who might harbor similar prejudices as part of their core values. Participants in the two dialogue roundtable sessions expressed their views that there are probably many more superintendents who have similar values. If this is the case, then we should try and understand more completely the mind-set of individuals who present one face publicly while internally harboring dramatically different core values.

Masks That Hide and Reveal

In his book *Emile*, French philosopher Jean Jacques Rousseau describes ways we view ourselves by using the terms *amour de soi* and *amour de propre*. *Amour de soi* is our authentic self—how we really see who we are. *Amour de propre*, on the other hand, is the way we want others to see us—masks that we often wear. Rousseau describes masks this way: "all men wear pretty much the same mask, but . . . there are faces more beautiful than the mask covering them."[11] Considering masks in this context can lead us to a sense of liberation if we can take off our masks and reveal something more beautiful underneath.

The reverse of this can also be true. An article in the *School Administrator* explained that "regarding the Coatesville texting crisis contains a graphic of a mask being removed that reveals a contorted, sinister, face behind a more benign mask."[12] Faces behind masks are not always more beautiful than the mask that hides them. Such is the case with the Coatesville racial incident.

Superintendent Como was a hero to many African American students and community members because of his role in coaching winning football teams. He was admired as the high school principal and later district superintendent. The texts revealed another person who, when communicating to his friend Donato, apparently did not feel bound by the social conventions that usually constrained him.

The same may be true of Donato. Both men removed their masks. Their true selves were revealed in the texts, and this revelation uncovered discord between each man's *amour de soi* and *amour de propre*. Their masks were fashioned from what they believed to be politically and socially correct behaviors and attitudes that were accepted in the context of their school community. Como and Donato apparently were friends—at least friendly enough to share these inner feelings.

Their morals appear to be isolated from the mainstream values of the learning communities that they served. Perhaps they never really examined their own core values relative to spiritual aspects of their being. Perhaps they never really examined them relative to the ones expressed in our founding documents—the Declaration of Independence and the United States Constitution—or to other universal documents such as the United Nations' Universal Declaration of Human Rights. To do this requires conscious efforts and should be considered at least as valuable to a person as their physical and intellectual well-being.

MIND, SPIRIT, BODY: A PATHWAY TO AUTHENTIC PERSONAL MEDITATION

Learning from the YMCA Tagline

Familiar to generations of Americans since it was introduced in 1891 is the tagline for the YMCA: "Mind, Spirit, Body." This expression advocates for individuals to live harmonious lives. Superintendents and other educational leaders are usually well schooled in the mind aspect of this triangle through their own education and required certifications. Many are also familiar with the benefits of regular exercise and good nutrition as a path to greater endurance and well-rounded physical health. To achieve personal harmony, however, they also need to develop the spiritual aspects of the triangle.

When the spiritual aspect of the triangle is nonexistent or weakened it makes it not only lopsided but also unstable and debilitating. Roger Joslin, in his book *Running the Spiritual Path*, integrates the physical and spiritual aspects of running. He writes that "the fully actualized human being can neglect neither body nor soul in his striving to become conscious and whole."[13] He writes further, "Remember that we are not merely human beings on a spiritual path, but we are spiritual beings on a human path."[14]

The spiritual side of the triangle can be explored through participation in organized religions. It can also be explored through various forms of meditation such as a vision quest (practiced by several native America tribes), Buddhist meditation, yoga, and the Spiritual Exercises of Saint Ignatius.

Some Forms of Personal Reflection and Meditation

Reflection on particular topics, practices, beliefs, and values usually means that an individual becomes more aware of them. Meditation, on the other hand, involves deep concentration involving a greater realization of the self in relation to an infinite universe expressed in a starry night sky, a walk in the woods on a wintry day, a sunset over a calm ocean, or the sweetness of a songbird seeking her or his mate.

Perhaps more significantly meditation can involve a greater realization of the self in relation to other beings. Insights and values gained from regular meditation can become integrated into the very core being of the participant. There are many variations of meditation. A powerful one is a Native American vision quest.

Vision quests usually involve individuals preparing their minds and bodies over a period of time to rid themselves of potentially harmful influences. Once they feel ready, they retreat to a private area, oftentimes on top of a mountain, where they fast for one or more days, empty themselves of earthly thoughts, connect with the greater universe, and hope to experience a spiritual awakening. Eagle Man from the Oglala Lakota tribe describes a vision quest this way:

> As each day goes by, the phases of life go through their cycles. At night, the stars come out. Pilades will actually dance for you if you're a vision quester. They light up, almost like a neon sign. I know people find that hard to believe, but that's just the mystery of the ceremony. An eagle will hover right over you knowing that you're in ceremony. Thunder and lightning come by, and you just endure it. It's no problem. Lightning can be flashing all around you, and you'll laugh. The Great Spirit is not going to take your life up there while you are vision questing.[15]

Another way to a fuller realization of the spiritual side of the "Y" triangle can be found in meditating on the four Buddhist sublime states of mind known as *Brahma-vihara*. These four states are equanimity, compassion, loving kindness, and sympathetic joy. They can form the foundation for a mind void of hatred as hatred is not compatible with these states. Benefits of deep meditation on them "will make these four qualities sink deep into the heart so that they become spontaneous attitudes not easily overthrown."[16]

Yoga meditation is another way of greatly enriching both a person's physical and spiritual well-being. It is built on centuries of tradition that aim to discover the unity of the self with the world and universe. Such meditation combines the ability to unify body and soul in seeking to find a richer fulfillment. In "A Beginner's Guide to Meditation," Maria Carico expresses yoga meditation as "an exquisite methodology [that] exists within the yoga tradition that is designed to reveal the interconnectedness of every living thing. This fundamental unity is referred to as advaita. Meditation is the actual experience of this union."[17]

Another powerful way to greater realization of the spiritual self can be found in the Jesuits' practice of the Spiritual Exercises of Saint Ignatius. For thirty days a participant in the Exercises meditates deeply on particular experiences and scenes in Jesus's life. There are several annotations of the thirty-day exercises. For example, one known as the 19th Annotation does not require thirty continuous days but instead one hour per day of meditation for twenty-four weeks.

An illustration of a meditation using the Spiritual Exercises follows. After reading John's New Testament account of Jesus's call to two of the first disciples, the participant might picture the time of day, feel the weather, breathe in the air, and imagine the river or dry land smells, hear the sounds of children and adults talking, and then listen to the words of Jesus when he said, "What are you looking for?" Their response was "Where do you live, Rabbi?" Jesus answered, "Come and see."[18] This scene can be imagined as a plain, powerful, and intimate dialogue. Jesus's invitation for the two to join him at his house for conversation and perhaps some tea, a glass of wine, or a beer both humanizes and spiritualizes this scene.

An Example of a Leader's Life in Harmony

An example of a leader whose has achieved a high degree of harmony between mind, body, and spirit is found in a Jesuit priest, Fr. Enrique Oizumi. He was a transformational leader in Bolivia of an educational movement known as *Fe y Alegria*.[19] Fe y Alegria is a Jesuit organization that runs schools for more than 260,000 students in one of the poorest countries in the hemisphere.

Fe y Alegria believes its mission is to build schools literally where the road ends. Many of them are in rural areas where students have to walk great distances, sometimes more than ten miles one way, which means they come to school on Monday mornings and return home on Friday afternoons.

In Fe y Alegria schools, teachers and administrators are paid the same meager salary as their colleagues in schools directly run by the government. However, a waiting list exists of government schools wanting to become part of Fe y Alegria. In large part this is because the schools are believed to be transformative for their populations.

The director, Fr. Oizumi, led them in a highly democratic way. He gave up a life of wealth to become a Jesuit. He later gave up a life of relative ease as head of a private school to become a parish priest in a native Aymara parish on the "El Alto" plain above La Paz. Here he learned the necessity of blending his beliefs with those of the indigenous population and focusing energies on a common mission: the education of children.

Oizumi has a leadership style that is greatly respected by central office colleagues, teachers in mud brick buildings, and students, as well as parents in poverty-stricken communities. He remains today part of a powerful flock in which he often learns more than he teaches. His spirituality is deep and renewed daily through meditation within a faith based on the Jesuit values of *cura personalis* (care of the person), *magis* (continuous quality improvement), and a strong belief in social justice in which "men and women are for others."[20]

Personal Reflection, Meditation, and Realization of Core Communal Values

Achieving a sense of personal harmony in the "Y" triangle is a lifelong quest. While this is unfolding, it is also important to consider one's core values relative to the greater communal society. Communal values are those that are generally recognized by the greater society and are usually accepted because they are part of our deepest philosophy as expressed in our founding documents. This can be facilitated by both reflecting and meditating on certain universal values that have emerged through our historical progression toward more complete democratic principles.

Whereas reflection indicates an awareness of certain values, meditation is more deep-seated and sustained, indicating a desire to become holistic with our being. Important touchstones in this evolution include the United States Declaration of Independence (1776), the United States Constitution (1789), the United States Bill of Rights (1791), the French Declaration of the Rights of Man and the Citizen (1793), and the Universal Declaration of Human Rights (1948).

Each of these important documents was born in the fire of war and washed with the blood of individuals seeking democracy and a greater sense of social justice. Elements common to these world-shaping documents include:

- equality;
- equal protection of laws;
- due process;
- freedom of religion, speech, press, and assembly;
- necessity of fair trials and lack of torture; and
- individual and collective security.

The United States Declaration of Independence is a keystone of our democracy. Thomas Jefferson and the committee with whom he wrote summarized the philosophy of John Locke its own way when they wrote, "We hold these truths to be self-evident, that all men [and women] are created equal. They are endowed by their Creator with certain unalienable rights. That among these are life, liberty, and the pursuit of happiness."[21]

In meditating on this famous expression an individual could begin by reading, if time permits, Carl Becker's *The Declaration of Independence: A Study on the History of Political Ideas.*[22] This would provide a rich context for a further deconstruction of the document. A person could also move directly to an examination of some key words or expressions without reading Becker's account of its formation. They could ask what they mean to them and whether or not they are part of their own core values.

For example, "we" resonates with the idea of community rather than the individual "I." "Truths" indicates something that is authentic and cannot be discarded. "Self-evident" signifies a truth that is obvious. "Created equal" is at the heart of John Locke's revolutionary philosophy (and subsequently Jefferson's) that power resides in the people—all of the people.

The first ten amendments to the United States Constitution are known as the Bill of Rights. Written by James Madison, they were a response to Anti-Federalists' views that such an enumeration of rights was needed to protect individual liberties. The first of these is generally considered the foundation safeguarding citizens' rights. It states, "Congress shall make no law respecting an establishment of religion, or prohibiting the free exercise thereof; or abridging the freedom of speech, or of the press; or the right of the people peaceably to assemble, and to petition the government for a redress of grievances."[23]

Deconstruction and meditation on these key rights would include an examination of an individual's tolerance for differing religious views, acceptance of diverse opinions of speech, and recognition of the important role of an independent press. Meditation should also include placing these rights in the current cultural and political context and determining if they are viable or if they are in danger of extinction.

The French Revolution, which began in 1789, eventually produced a Declaration of the Rights of Man that is similar to the United States Bill of Rights. There were several versions introduced during the revolution that showed an evolution of French political thinking during that time. Of interest is the French Declaration of the Rights of Man and the Citizen (1793) because number thirty-four summarizes a core theme of social justice as follows: "There is oppression against the social body when a single one of its members is oppressed; there is oppression against each member when the social body is oppressed."[24]

Though this version was never formally adopted, the philosophy expressed in these words is an important hallmark of French philosophy and political thinking to this day. Meditation on these words would solicit questions regarding the extent of social justice that an individual has as part of his or her core values.

The United Nations adopted the Universal Declaration of Human Rights (Universal Declaration) on December 10, 1948. It grew from the horrors of World War II when the world's soul was laid bare by the Axis atrocities. Especially horrifying were the Nazi death camps and other Gestapo imprisonments.[25] Eleanor Roosevelt chaired a special drafting committee for the Universal Declaration to expand on the Four Freedoms, which were the goals for the Allies during the war: freedom of speech, freedom of religion, freedom from fear, and freedom from want.[26]

Educational leaders may find number twenty-six of the Universal Declaration particularly interesting as it states, "Education shall be directed to the full development of the human personality and to the strengthening of respect for human rights and fundamental freedoms . . . [and] shall promote understanding, tolerance and friendship among all nations, racial or religious groups, and shall further the activities of the United Nations for the maintenance of peace."[27]

Individual meditation on this right may include an examination of educational realities in both the United States and the world, which would include identification of areas where this right is not fully manifested such as equity of educational funding and resources. Another may include a consideration of historical and current immigration policies of the United Sates relative to "understanding, tolerance and friendship among all nations, racial or religious groups."

Another valuable meditation can focus on certain aspects of the historical context that led to the Universal Declaration. Polish composer Henryk Górecki's Symphony No. 3 provides rich material for this as it grew from the horrors of war and the occupation of subjected people. Górecki wrote this symphony in 1976 and, though it was not well received at first, today it is known to millions of people by its subtitle, "Symphony of Sorrowful Songs."

The second movement is both powerful and poignant because the words that accompany the orchestra are those written on a Gestapo cellar wall by an eighteen-year-old-girl who was imprisoned there. Before signing her name, she wrote, "No, mother, do not weep, most chaste Queen of Heaven, support me always."[28]

Words of the third movement are from a Polish folksong lamenting a mother's loss of her son, who vanishes following an uprising:

> He lies in his grave
> And I know not where
> Though I keep asking people
> Everywhere
>
> . . .
>
> Oh, sing for him
> God's little song-birds
> Since his mother
> Cannot find him
>
> And you, God's little flowers
> May you blossom all around
> So that my son
> May sleep happily.[29]

Reading these words while listening to the music can produce powerful emotions and raise serious considerations regarding personal core values on the worthiness of all human lives. It also focuses on the historical evil realities of Nazism and the horrors and injustices of war.

Self-Test on Integrity of Personal Core Communal Values—Or May I Wear My Hat?

Growing up in Cleveland, Ohio, in the early 1950s meant that you were an Indians baseball fan. The team was considered among the best in the history of baseball, having won 111 games in 1954. But then they lost the World Series in four straight games to the New York Giants.

The disappointment at the series loss did not seem to diminish the stylized grin of "Chief Wahoo," whose image appeared on personal items such as hats, shirts, and jackets as well as on public and private buildings, bridges, and individual homes. It was only later that the image was considered harmful to Native Americans. More on the chief is considered in chapter 3, where the image is part of a powerful learning experience.

The setting for a good self-test regarding the integrity of your core values is to imagine yourself as a kid who grew up in Cleveland during the World Series fever. In later years you realized the chief's demeaning grin was offensive to Native Americans who regularly protested the team logo outside the ball stadium. Three questions:

1. Would you continue to wear your Chief Wahoo hat if there was a chance that you would meet any Native Americans?

2. Would you wear your hat if you were with a group of friends at a cabin in the woods?
3. Would you wear your hat if you were alone for a long walk deep in the woods?

How you answer can be an indicator of the integrity of your core values relative to the values of equality and worthiness of all persons no matter their race, ethnicity, or religious creed. Recognizing that at times we all wear masks, ask yourself: Do I regularly wear a mask, sometimes wear a partial mask, or usually wear no mask? Once you feel comfortable with your degree of self-honesty, it is time to expand meditation on communal values to include your faculty, leadership team, groups of students, and/or various segments of the greater community.

COLLECTIVE MEDITATION, CONFLICTS, AND REALIZATION OF CORE COMMUNAL VALUES

Professional development for school administrators, teachers, other staff members, and community groups often consists of one-shot sessions that impart information and, occasionally, inspiration. Oftentimes such information and inspiration last only as long as the sessions themselves. Faculty and other meetings frequently entail principals or superintendents presenting prepared material imposed on them from outside sources.

These sessions do little to build a sense of community and deny the professionalism of participants. Consideration of core communal values relative to our national philosophy as expressed in our founding documents can dramatically change the dynamics of professional development.

Educational leaders need to reflect and meditate on core communal values privately. More importantly, they need to build communities of learners who meditate on them collectively. Building such communities is critically important for the well-being of our democracy considering the current emphasis on standardized testing that either diminishes or eliminates the teaching of communal values through social studies from many of our schools. [30]

As previously presented, some of the same key words and phrases from the United States Declaration of Independence (1776), the United States Constitution (1789), the United States Bill of Rights (1791), the French Declaration of the Rights of Man and the Citizen (1793), and the Universal Declaration of Human Rights (1948) can be used for collective reflection and eventually meditation. A further review of the importance of these documents is considered in a different context in chapter 3.

Simply reflecting on communal values is not sufficient to creating schools that honor those values. They need to be institutionalized by communities of learners who share those values.

Resources for Direct Action

Once a community of learners has sufficiently dialogued the importance of core communal values, it is ready to move to some direct action projects. One example could be curriculum development projects regarding racial hatred designed for particular grades, subjects, or entire schools. This would mean securing and using resources that can help achieve positive human relations outcomes. Among them are the examples found in textbox 1.1.

Textbox 1.1

- The Anti-Defamation League provides anti-bias curricula resources and interactive training programs for educators at www.adl.org.
- The Council on American-Islamic Relations offers a series of guides to explain Muslim religious practices to educators at www.caor.com.
- The Pennsylvania Human Relations Commission educates both educators and students on civil rights at phrc.pa.gov.
- The United Nations Human Rights Council offers publications and resources supporting human rights education at www.ohchr.org/ED/PublicationsResources/Pages/TrainingEducation.aspx.
- The Southern Poverty Law Center provides Teaching Tolerance educational kits and free subscriptions to its educator's magazine at www.splcenter.org.
- BaFa' BaFa' offers an interactive simulation that is designed to provide diversity training for educators at https://www.simulationtrainingsystems.com.

These resources are diverse and provide a foundation for direct collective meditation as well as for preparing a diversity curriculum for students. They can also help answer questions about the national and local political culture that often exposes hatred inherent in radical fringe groups such as neo-Nazis or the Ku Klux Klan. The Southern Poverty Law center estimates that there were approximately 917 active hate groups in the United States in 2017.[31] A description of a neo-Nazi group's attempts to infiltrate a school district's student body as well as a successful resistance to it is presented in chapter 2.

SUMMARY

The raw racist texts from supposedly trusted school leaders—a superintendent and an athletic director—upended a school district and posed serious questions regarding their core values. Some insight for such actions might be found by considering the masks that everyone wears at times and the real faces that they hide. The racist texts exposed the leaders' inner core values and led to their losing their jobs and reputations.

Some possible ways to help avoid such a crisis include considering the YMCA tagline that connects mind, body, and spirit. Maintaining a healthy body and an active mind is often part of a leader's lifestyle. Of lesser importance to many is creating and nourishing a rich spiritual life. This chapter suggests that having all three is critically important and that a pathway to spiritual well-being can be found in both reflection and meditation. Whereas reflection brings greater awareness, meditation can lead to a more authentic realization of basic core values regarding the worthiness of all individuals.

Once core personal values are secure, leaders can move to meditation of core communal values common to Americans as expressed in our founding documents as well as those from other democratic societies. Such reflection and meditation on core democratic values can form the basis for insightful and powerful professional development sessions for teachers and other members of the school community. These actions can realize the belief stated in this chapter's opening quotation that leadership springs from within.

Racial hatred is often at the center of beliefs expressed by neo-Nazi hate groups. Attempts to recruit new high school student members into the racist cult known as the "Pottstown SS" are the subject of the next chapter.

NOTES

1. Chris Lowney, *Heroic Leadership* (Chicago: Loyola Press, 2003), 15.

2. Ibid., 20.

3. Ibid., 9.

4. Michael Price and Kristina Scala, "CASD in Crisis after Racially-Charged Text Messages Surface," *Daily Local News*, September 22, 2013, 1.

5. Note: the "n" word is spelled out in the original quotation.

6. Note: text language for "laughing my a** off.

7. School Digger, Coatesville Area School District, http://www.schooldigger.com/go/PA/schools/0624005012/school.aspx (accessed January 26, 2016).

8. Michael Price and Kristina Scala, "Coatesville School Board Allows 2 Execs to Resign after Racist Texts; Public Fumes," *Daily Local News*, September 25, 2013, 1.

9. Private communication from a high school counselor to Terrance Furin, February 3, 2014.

10. This book's author chaired the roundtables at both the Pennsylvania Association of School Administrators' and the American Association of School Administrators' conferences. Comments are based on notes taken from those conferences.

11. Jean-Jacques Rousseau, *Emile, or On Education*, ed. and trans. Allan Bloom (New York: Basic Books, 1979), 237.

12. Terrance Furin, "Combating Hatred Among Us," *School Administrator* (November 2017): 43.

13. Roger Joslin, *Running the Spiritual Path* (New York: St. Martin's Griffin, 2003), 230.

14. Ibid., 231.

15. Ed McGaa, "Eagle Man," Eagle Man's Vision Quest, http://native-americans-online.com/native-american-vision-quest.html (accessed December 5, 2017).

16. Nyanaponika Thera, "The Four Sublime States, Contemplations on Love, Compassion, Sympathetic Joy, and Equanimity," https://www.accesstoinsight.org/lib/authors/nyanaponika/wheel006.html (accessed December 5, 2017).

17. Maria Carico, "A Beginner's Guide to Meditation," https://www.yogajournal.com/meditation/let-s-meditate (accessed December 5, 2017).

18. John 1: 37–39, *Good News New Testament* (New York: American Bible Society, 1976).

19. The description of Fr. Oizumi is a firsthand account as this author worked with Fr. Oizumi and Fe y Alegria schools periodically for approximately four years beginning in 2003 both in Bolivia and in the United States. Fr. Oizumi left the leadership of Fe y Alegria in 2006.

20. George W. Traub, "Do you Speak Ignatian?" (Xavier University, Cincinnati: 2002), https://www.siprep.org/uploaded/about_si/documents/Do_You_Speak_Ignatian.pdf (accessed December 10, 2017).

21. The United States Declaration of Independence, https://www.archives.gov/founding-docs/declaration-transcript (accessed December 5, 2017).

22. Carl Becker, *The Declaration of Independence: A Study on the History of Political Ideas* (New York: Harcourt, Brace and Co., 1922).

23. Bill of Rights of the United States of America (1791), http://www.billofrightsinstitute.org/founding-documents/bill-of-rights/ (accessed December 11, 2017).

24. Declaration of the Rights of Man and Citizen from the Constitution of Year I (1793), Frank Maloy Anderson, ed., *The Constitutions and Other Select Documents Illustrative of the History of France 1789–1901* (Minneapolis: H. W. Wilson, 1904), reprinted in Jack R. Censer and Lynn Hunt, eds., *Liberty, Equality, Fraternity: Exploring the French Revolution* (American Social History Productions, 2001), http://www.columbia.edu/~iw6/docs/dec1793.html (accessed December 5, 2017).

25. United for Human Rights, Universal Declaration of Human Rights, http://www.humanrights.com/what-are-human-rights/universal-declaration-of-human-rights/ (accessed December 13, 2017).

26. For an elaboration on these four freedoms that were presented in a speech by President Franklin Roosevelt on January 6, 1941, see https://www.google.com/search?q=Four+Freedoms&spell=1&sa=X&ved=0ahUKEwiQ_cHhqofYAhXIQCYKHTl9AT0QBQgmKAA&biw=1600&bih=769.

27. Universal Declaration of Human Rights, http://www.un.org/en/universal-declaration-human-rights/ (accessed December 13, 2017).

28. Words Accompanying Górecki's Symphony No. 3, https://web.ics.purdue.edu/~felluga/holocaust/goreckilyrics696.html (accessed December 13, 2017).

29. Ibid.

30. Fifth-grade teachers in a Philadelphia elementary school were told by their principal not to teach social studies from October until April and to use the scheduled social studies time to concentrate on math instead because the benchmark standardized tests showed a deficiency. In conversations with several educators since this was communicated to the author in an e-mail from a fifth-grade teacher, Freeden Oeurr (December 20, 2004), this practice appears not to be an anomaly.

31. Southern Poverty Law Center, "Hate Groups," https://www.splcenter.org/hate-map (accessed December 5, 2017).

Chapter Two

Combating a Neo-Nazi Hate Group

Sieg Heil to the Aryan race and to those who are willing to fight and die for it![1]

As with the phoenix who is reborn in fire, so the Pottstown S.S. rises from the ashes left behind by their fore bearers to create a new and better elite force to serve the Aryan cause.[2]

This chapter's opening quotations are taken from a neo-Nazi recruitment flyer that was distributed throughout the Owen J. Roberts school district in early April 1994. The flyer called for a student boycott on May 6 to commemorate the anniversary of the death of Heinrich Himmler, Adolph Hitler's assistant and head of the dreaded Nazi SS. The group who claimed responsibility for distributing the flyer was known as the Pottstown SS. It was attempting to recruit new members from high school and middle school students in the rural/suburban district of approximately 3,800 students located approximately forty miles from Philadelphia.

The Owen J. Roberts school district covers approximately 108 square miles in bucolic northern Chester County, Pennsylvania. This is a prosperous area and one of the fastest growing in the region. It is known for pastoral settings of open space and rolling countryside. Drive thirty minutes to the south and you are in some of Philadelphia's emerging affluent suburbs. The same distance to the east is historic Valley Forge. To the west is Amish country, where the nineteenth-century sounds of horses' hooves remind us of a peaceful past era. To the north, approaching the Lehigh Valley, the landscape looks similarly peaceful. This belies the hatred that occurred here in the 1990s on a compound dedicated to the training of neo-Nazis.

In April 1994, Mark Thomas's compound near Seisholtzville in Berks County was anything but peaceful. It was there that Thomas hosted a weekend Hitler Youth Festival attended by approximately two hundred neo-Nazis and other white supremacists.[3] The Pottstown SS was formed from this group, and inspiration for the distribution of recruitment flyers and the proposed boycott came from this rally.

This chapter describes a confrontation between members of the Owen J. Roberts community and the neo-Nazis. It contains a scholar-practitioner section that explains the emergence of a public pedagogy that turned the entire community into a classroom. This pedagogy grew from a series of dialogue groups that had been established in the district. These dialogues, aimed at developing a common educational philosophy, were based on the child-centered progressive theories of John Dewey. Dewey considered teachers, along with parents, to be the most significant people in a child's education. The role of teachers as key decision makers helped to turn the confrontation with the neo-Nazis into a teachable moment that became a learning opportunity for the entire community.

CONFRONTATION

A Neo-Nazi Recruitment Flyer

The peaceful quiet that often accompanies the warming of a mid-April morning in the school district was broken harshly when several alarmed high school students arrived at school with neo-Nazi flyers. The flyers were designed to recruit new members into a hate group calling itself the Pottstown SS. The group attempted a show of strength by demanding that students boycott all of the district's schools on May 6 to commemorate the anniversary of Heinrich Himmler's death.

The flyer contains a rough drawing of Himmler, former chief of the German Gestapo and head of the SS. It includes twin thunder/lightning bolts meant to replicate the dreaded SS insignia. Himmler is flanked by two swastikas, a symbol known to many ancient cultures that under Hitler and the Nazis became the symbol of white Aryan power and horrific brutality. Beneath the drawing is a hand-scrawled statement that proclaimed the organization's goal was to "give Aryan men who truly believe in their race the opportunity to fight to keep their race safe and strong, even if it means their deaths in the process."[4]

In this dramatic way, one of a school district's most dreaded nightmares—a community upheaval fed by rampant rumors and fears of violence against students—became a reality.

Questions Abound

The switchboard lit up as news of the flyers and the impending boycott quickly spread throughout the district. Teachers were looking for direction on what to tell their students. Central office administrators asked them to remain calm and quickly assured them through e-mails and personal school visits that district security plans would ensure the safety of students and staff members. These same administrators also knew that even the best plans are not always successful.

Calls from staff members were followed by others from frantic parents and citizens. They wanted to know answers to myriad questions. What did the school administration know about the neo-Nazi group that was distributing the flyers? How do hate groups recruit members? Was this threat real and what could be expected in the way of violence? Would classes be canceled? If schools remained open, how could administrators and teachers guarantee the safety of all students? What could the community do to keep groups such as this from disrupting its schools?

Policies were in place to deal with immediate safety and security concerns. These were not sufficient, however, to answer the questions coming from all sides. The district did not have a strategy to keep a hate group from establishing a lasting presence in the school community. There were approximately two weeks before the boycott. This provided time to develop a blueprint to deal with the impending crisis.

A Crisis Blueprint

The day after the flyers appeared, the district's leadership team discussed ways of dealing with the imminent crisis. First and foremost it reviewed the district's security plans. This was followed by launching a thorough communication plan to keep all constituencies fully informed of actions in dealing with the emergency.

The communication plan included announcements, mailings, and public media information provided to students, parents, religious leaders, government officials, and general community members. These are prudent measures usually taken in dealing with such situations. District teachers and administrators wanted to do more. They recognized the emergency as a significant opportunity to lead the district in confronting raw hatred and bigotry. With this end in mind, they contacted the Pennsylvania Human Relations Commission for advice.

As chance would have it, one of the commission's experts on intolerance, Ann Van Dyke, was scheduled to come to the school district that week to give a culminating presentation to the high school faculty who were engaged in a series of dialogue sessions regarding human rights issues. These sessions were part of multiyear district-wide staff development programs aimed at developing a common philosophy by reading several books and conducting dialogues regarding their meanings and practical applications.

Accompanied by a human rights specialist from the Pennsylvania State Police, Van Dyke began the high school dialogue session by informing teachers that Pennsylvania led the nation that year with forty-four active hate groups. She informed the group that the neo-Nazi organization known as the Pottstown SS was unknown to her and appeared to be a relatively small organization.

Large or small was not the issue. She explained that violence can come in any size and then described the serious problems that a nearby school district was having in confronting the Keystone Knights, a local affiliate of the Ku Klux Klan. Distressed by this information, teachers asked the big question: How does a school district combat this hatred and keep such groups from establishing themselves in a community?

Van Dyke began to answer the question by leading the group through an insightful two-page newsletter titled "How Hate Groups Recruit Our Young People" prepared by Floyd Cochran, a former propaganda minister of a white supremacist group known as Church of Jesus Christ Christian/Aryan Nations. Cochran had been involved in various racist movements for more than twenty years and left the Church of Jesus Christ Christian/Aryan Nations only after his son was born with a cleft palate and his superiors told him that he was now considered racially inferior. Angered, he did an about-face and began to use his inside knowledge of hate group operations to inform young people of their dangers.

In his newsletter, prepared for the Montana Office of Public Instruction, Cochran addressed the basic human need of belonging. He wrote that on entering the movement he felt as if he was part of not only a family but also a movement that was important and larger than he was. He indicated that many young racists come from dysfunctional families. Most are alienated from school. They look elsewhere to fulfill their need to belong. He wrote that hate groups are there waiting for them. [5]

Professional Advice

After reviewing Floyd Cochran's newsletter, Ann Van Dyke described actions that had proven successful in other communities that had encountered hate groups. She referenced several points from a document of hers titled "So Now What Do You Do?" Her advice included:

• forming a unity coalition and defining the community as one that honors unity, tolerance, and diversity;

- redirecting energy and attention to positive community events that build harmony among citizens;
- ensuring that the school district has a multicultural curriculum and cultural awareness training for all staff members;
- establishing an ongoing adult education program that includes religious, civic, and other community groups; and
- listening to youth and including them in planning various school and community activities. [6]

   Several of her points formed the blueprint for actions led by the district's high school teachers.

Teachers Lead the Way in Avoiding a Crisis

A series of dialogue sessions throughout the district had become the heart of a professional development program designed to aid teachers in becoming both the chief architects as well as implementers of the district's curriculum. A majority of the high school teachers were involved in dialogue sessions during the 1993–94 school year that were aimed at developing an interdisciplinary curriculum based on encounters with intolerance. Some of the materials for these sessions were Stanley Elkin's book *Slavery*, Elie Wiesel's *The Night Trilogy*, and Steven Spielberg's movie *Schindler's List*. In addition to dialogue sessions held at the high school, participants visited the Holocaust museum in Washington.

   As a result of these dialogue sessions, many teachers felt an increased sensitivity toward human rights issues. They decided to take the lead in mobilizing teachers throughout the district and planned activities to take place on the day of the proposed boycott. These included developing classroom lessons on hate group dynamics and human rights issues that were designed for high school and middle school students at whom both neo-Nazi recruitment and the boycott were aimed.

   Teachers also organized a no putdown day complete with suggested activities and buttons for all staff and students. These were especially valuable for elementary students as it opened up discussions on various levels that dealt with intolerance and the need to be respectful of individual differences. Primary students, for example, discussed the value of individuality and ways to respect those who are different. They talked about different ways to avoid conflicts in classrooms, on playgrounds, and in neighborhood settings. The neo-Nazis had provided a powerful teachable moment that led to substantive discussions that might otherwise not have happened.

   Teacher leadership was crucial in planning these activities and proved to be important in soothing community uneasiness. Most teachers were well known and respected by the majority of parents. They became trusted communicators. Their presence along with administrators and police outside of their schools on the morning of the boycott proved to be a deciding factor in calming fears and quelling the boycott.

For all practical purposes the boycott fizzled. Attendance at the schools was nearly normal with a slight dip recorded at the high school. Many students later provided an explanation for this when they admitted the boycott gave them a great opportunity to skip school on a sunny spring day. Many also made it clear that their absence was not intended as a show of support for the neo-Nazis. Once the initial crisis passed without incident, it became possible for teachers, administrators, school board members, and students to begin to implement some of the long-range plans based on the points shared by Ann Van Dyke at the high school dialogue session.

Building for the Future

Ann Van Dyke gave two key pointers to keep hate groups from establishing a foothold in a community:

- Form a unity coalition and define your community as one that honors unity, tolerance, and diversity.
- Redirect energy and attention to positive community events that build harmony among citizens.

Forming a unity coalition became a central focus, and more than 150 parents, students, and community representatives attended a meeting that was designed to form one. At the meeting teachers and administrators led small group discussions that focused on the information regarding hate group dynamics provided by the Pennsylvania Human Rights Commission. Attendance remained strong at several other sessions that were held throughout that year.

It is not easy to measure the long-term effects that this neo-Nazi threat had on this school community. There were no pre- or post-tests, no statistics to validate the success or failure of actions taken, and no benchmarks or percentages to measure progress. This may be troubling in a society that increasingly relies on statistics to prove the success of educational initiatives. What did emerge was a greater awareness of hate groups and their attempts to strike out at both schools and society in general. From this grew a public pedagogy as a means of dealing with such issues.

The emergence of this pedagogy was remarkable considering the history and demographics of this school district. It made local and regional headlines four years earlier regarding school prayer at commencement when the Jewish valedictorian was granted a restraining order against prayer at the ceremony.

As described in chapter 5, this caused an uproar in the community that seemed to support very conservative social values.

The neo-Nazi confrontation revealed a different set of social values within the community. One example was the formation of an educational foundation dedicated to human rights issues. The formation of the foundation demonstrated an awareness regarding the potential danger of hate groups. It was also an example of a powerful public pedagogy at work.

The Owen J. Roberts Education Foundation

The Owen J. Roberts Education Foundation, complete with bylaws and a board of directors representing a cross section of the community, became a reality within a few months of the proposed neo-Nazi boycott. Its first major function was to plan an event designed to bring together citizens, parents, and students to honor the district's namesake, Owen J. Roberts.

Owen J. Roberts was a former justice of the U.S. Supreme Court who often supported important human rights issues such as opposition to the relocation of Japanese Americans during World War II. Although Roberts was a former resident of the community and a member of the board of education that had voted to unify seven separate school districts into one, many people did not know about his important role in human rights issues.

For this reason the Owen J. Roberts Education Foundation board decided to place its initial focus on providing a greater knowledge of his life and significant activities. The date for a commemoration of Roberts's life was purposefully chosen to coincide with the first anniversary of the proposed neo-Nazi boycott.

More than seven hundred parents and community members attended a Sunday afternoon program that memorialized Owen J. Roberts through the screening of a video of historical events regarding his life that was produced by school district personnel. This event triggered a fund-raising campaign that netted more than twenty thousand dollars for the foundation during its first year. The money established annual human rights seminars for students, teachers, and community members to coincide with the anniversary date of the boycott. The first featured speaker was Floyd Cochran, the former member of the Church of Jesus Christ Christian/Aryan Nations.

Floyd Cochran's powerful lessons to middle school and high school students during the day were a prelude to his evening presentation to more than five hundred citizens. Special security guards were needed as his life had been threatened by members of his former Aryan Nations hate group. He stunned listeners as he described his role in recruitment activities and the violent acts he committed against minorities. Cochran's work on the advisory board of the Pennsylvania Alliance for Democracy as well as the education staff of the Liberty Museum and Education Center in Philadelphia is known by hundreds who have seen evidence of his advocacy for important human rights causes.

The Owen J. Roberts Education Foundation continued for several years emphasizing human rights issues that emerged from the proposed neo-Nazi boycott. It continues to this day with its mission broadened to include fundraising to advance the overall goals of the school district. Its initial formation demonstrates the institutionalization of an important democratic process in which teachers and other school leaders served as a catalyst in bringing together citizens from seven different townships to discuss important issues of tolerance and respect for basic human rights.

In these ways school personnel once again engaged the community on the serious issues of student alienation, hatred, and potential violence. This example of public pedagogy may not have happened had it not been for the successful confrontation with the neo-Nazis four years earlier.

The confrontation with neo-Nazis in the Owen J. Roberts school district did not make national news. The proposed boycott did make it onto the front page of the most popular local paper, the *Pottstown Mercury*, where the headlines proclaimed "Riot Rumor Keeps Students Home."[7] As with many disasters, the story captured momentary angst. Once the crisis was past the issue faded from the instant news and from many peoples' memories. Just because it is not immediate news does not mean that the threats have vanished.

According to the Southern Poverty Law Center (SPLC), 917 active hate groups operated in the United States in 2017. The center defines hate groups as organizations that hold beliefs and carry out practices that attack or malign an entire class of people. Prominent on the SPLC list are the Ku Klux Klan and the Neo-Confederates. While these groups have their base in the former Confederacy, others operate north of the Mason Dixon Line. They are known by various names associated with neo-Nazis, racist skinheads, white nationalists, Aryan Nation, and other white supremacist groups.[8]

The SPLC is only one national organization that can be helpful in providing information or advice on dealing with hate groups. There are other resources and strategies that can also be useful for school leaders faced with combating hatred from these groups.

Helpful Resources and a Summary of Strategies in Dealing with Hate Groups

These are some resources that can be helpful to school leaders as they combat radical hate groups.

Textbox 2.1

- The Southern Poverty Law Center, organized in 1971, is nationally recognized in confronting hate groups. It can be accessed at https://www.splcenter.org/ or by writing to the Southern Poverty Law Center, 400 Washington Ave., Montgomery, AL, 36104, or by calling (toll free) 888-414-7752.
- The Anti-Defamation League, founded in 1913 by B'nai B'rith in New York City, is nationally prominent in combating bias and hate crimes. Its *Blueprint for Action* can be accessed at http://www.adl.org/combating_hate/. See the website for regional addresses and phone numbers.
- The Center for Democratic Renewal was founded in 1979. It is a national organization that deals with racism and white supremacy. Its publication *When Hate Groups Come to Town: A Manual of Effective Community Responses* is helpful in dealing with hate groups. The Center can be accessed at https://www.sourcewatch.org/index.php/Center_for_Democratic_Renewal or by writing to the Center for Democratic Renewal, P.O. Box 50469, Atlanta, GA, 30302, or by calling 404-221-0035.
- The Pennsylvania Human Relations Commission is one of numerous human relations commissions that exist in nearly every state. It can be accessed at http://www.phrc.state.pa.us/ or by writing to the Pennsylvania Human Relations Commission, 110 N. 8th Street, Philadelphia, PA, 19107, or by calling 215-560-2496.
- The National Council for the Social Studies, founded in 1921, is the largest association dedicated to social studies education. It has numerous resources dealing with multiculturalism and social studies curricula. It can be accessed at http://www.ncss.org/ or by writing to the National Council for the Social Studies, 8555 Sixteenth St., Silver Spring, MD, 20910.
- The National Multi Cultural Institute, founded in 1983, is a nationally recognized organization that provides training in multiculturalism. It can be accessed at http://www.nmci.org/ or by writing to the National Multi Cultural Institute, 595 6th Street, Brooklyn, NY, 11215.

The best preparation for confronting hate groups begins long before a crisis hits the community. These are some useful strategies for school leaders to follow before an emergency develops:

- Ensure that the mission, policies, and curriculum of the school district include multiculturalism and social justice ideals.
- Create a unity of purpose and follow democratic decision making among the district's administrators, teachers, and support staff so that when a crisis develops one person is not alone in confronting it.
- Develop substantive connections with parents as well as the community's civic and religious leaders through participation in PTA/PTOs, service organizations, chambers of commerce, and religious groups.
- Create positive relationships with local media personnel representing newspapers as well as TV and radio stations.
- Ensure that the district has a variety of ways for communicating with the staff, students, parents, and greater community that include newsletters, websites, emergency calling/text messaging chains, and social media and update as often as possible.
- Review security policies and make certain that mechanics are in place for dealing with emergencies that include contact information with law enforcement personnel and human relations commissions.

When a crisis hits a community, school leaders might find these steps helpful:

- Assemble the administrative team and their closest advisers to determine an immediate course of action.
- Seek advice from law enforcement agencies as well as state or local human relations commissions that deal with hate crimes.
- Inform board members, district staff, students, parents, and the greater community of the crisis as well as actions planned to deal with it.
- Review and if necessary put in place emergency plans for dealing with the crisis.

After the immediate crisis has passed school leaders may want to lead the schools in creating a lasting public pedagogy with the community. These tips may be helpful:

- Form unity coalitions representing a broad range of parents, students, and community representatives to educate various constituencies regarding hate group dynamics.
- Establish adult education programs that engage religious, civic, and other community groups regarding hate group dynamics as well as other human relations issues.
- Review the district's practices to ensure that a social studies curriculum includes multiculturalism, social justice, and hate group dynamics.

The preceding sections of this chapter have detailed the practical aspects of a school district and community that successfully confronted a neo-Nazi threat. One major reason for their success was the role that teachers played in both confronting the crisis and helping to develop a public pedagogy that moved beyond school's walls and educated citizens of the greater community.

Teachers assumed leadership positions in large part because of a democratic management philosophy that recognized the importance of teachers and placed them with students in the center of the organizational structure. It is important for practitioners to understand the theoretical perspectives that place teachers at the center of a democratically organized school district. It is also important for them to understand that these same perspectives form the basis for development of public pedagogy.

CREATING COMMUNITIES OF LEARNERS: THE CRITICAL IMPORTANCE OF TEACHERS

Central Role of the Classroom Teacher in a Democratically Organized School District

John Dewey's progressive philosophy begins with the student. Next to the student the most important person in creating a child-centered, dynamic educational environment is the classroom teacher. Theirs is a symbiotic relationship, each dependent on the other for growth and learning.

Figure 2.1 shows a typical school district organizational chart that places teachers at the bottom where the weight of all those above presses on them and turns them into little more than cogs in some illusory giant machine. Students are not listed at all on many similar charts. Figure 2.2 places students (with parents) and teachers at the center of the district's organization and shows power flowing both inward and outward. The second conceptualization is considerably more consistent with Dewey's progressive philosophy.

Dewey recognized this relationship when he established his laboratory school in 1896. Educational historian and theorist Lawrence Cremin described this school as "the most interesting experimental venture in American education; indeed, there are those who insist that there has been nothing since to match it in excitement, quality, and contribution."[9]

To be a teacher in Dewey's school was extremely demanding. Laurel Tanner, an educational writer who has studied Dewey's laboratory school, wrote that "clearly the teachers were professionals, not mechanical toys or technicians."[10] Tanner defined professionalism as embodying both intellectual freedom and responsibility. Both of these factors need to be present if teachers are to develop an engaging curriculum. Maxine Greene, prominent

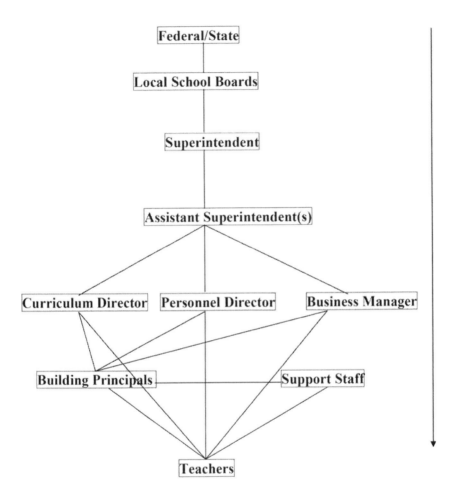

Figure 2.1.   Traditional School District Organizational Chart

educational theorist and former pupil of John Dewey, believes that in a school that honors these principles teachers are more likely to, in her words, "do philosophy."[11]

No one evokes images as ennobling of the teaching profession as does Maxine Greene. There are numerous examples of these images in her book *Teacher as Stranger.* Consider this illustration. After describing life-changing challenges presented by poet Rainer Maria Rilke's poem "Torso of an

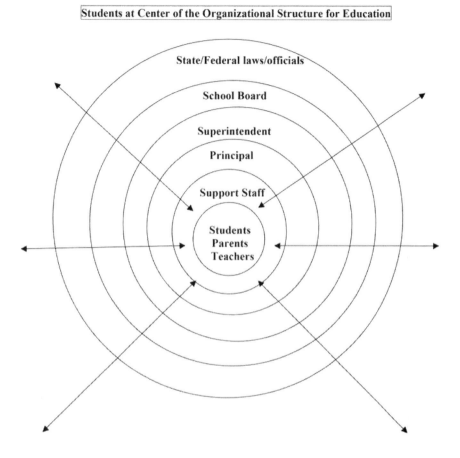

Students at Center of the Organizational Structure for Education

State/Federal laws/officials

School Board

Superintendent

Principal

Support Staff

Students
Parents
Teachers

Figure 2.2. Students at Center of the Organizational Structure for Education

Archaic Apollo" vis-à-vis Auguste Rodin's sculpture of Apollo, she draws a comparison between their work and a teacher's:

> The teacher can find an analogy here, since his very project involves making that demand. He is also engaged in transmuting and illuminating material to the end of helping others see afresh. If he is able to think what he is doing while he is vitally present as a person, he may arouse others to act on their own freedom. Learning to learn, some of those persons may move beyond the sheltered places until they stand by their own choice in the high wind of thought.[12]

This description truly is "teacher as stranger"—or looking at students and their society through new eyes. More importantly, it represents teachers as professionals. If we are ever to realize an ideal in education wherein the role of the teacher is to inspire others to "move beyond the sheltered places until they stand by their own choice in the high wind of thought," then teachers must be at the center of power—at the core of the organizational structure. It is here that they can exercise intellectual freedom and develop the responsibility that accompanies it. This demands a democratic organization that seamlessly supports teachers as professionals. It requires that teachers are involved in making fundamental decisions regarding the education of each student.

Teachers as Decision Makers

The key decisions in which teachers in a democratically organized school district should actively be involved include helping to define the educational mission, developing the curriculum to implement the mission, establishing the standards that emerge from the curriculum, constructing the tests that measure the effectiveness of the curriculum, and designing the classroom pedagogy to teach the curriculum. Other important areas for teacher involvement include professional development, design of the educational environment, and community outreach.

Being involved in fundamental decisions does not mean being involved in every decision. There are times, even in a democratically organized district, when it is better for administrators to use authoritative rather than democratic processes. Some of these include implementation of policies, the budget, and security plans; organizing support services (transportation, food services, building maintenance); and constructing master schedules and securing books, materials, and other supplies. Deciding when teachers should be involved in decision making often presents dilemmas, conflicts, and confusion for school leaders.

A consideration of above- and below-the-line activities relative to teacher professional involvement, as presented in figure 2.3, may help to resolve some of that confusion.

Those items above the line require substantive teacher involvement as they are the heart of the educational enterprise. Below-the-line functions should be the primary responsibility of the school administration. This does not mean that they are unimportant functions. It does mean that they need to be managed as efficiently as possible to avoid chaos and dangerous situations.

When operating below-the-line school principals, assistant principals, district superintendents, and others are considered administrators or managers. Once below-the-line functions are firmly in place, administrators need to move above the line and become colleagues with teachers in development of the most important educational functions.

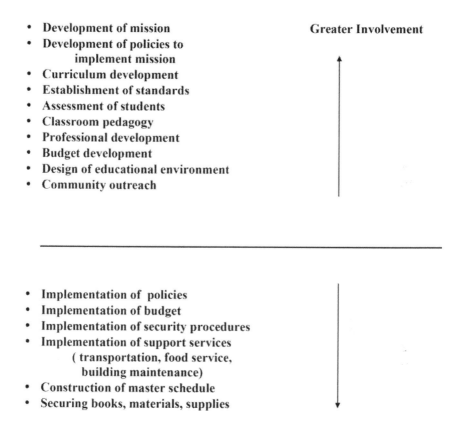

Figure 2.3.   Above- and Below-the-Line Activities Related to Teacher Involvement

Another revealing way of viewing the importance of teacher involvement in above-the-line activities is to integrate it relative to three well-known educational theories: Douglas McGregor's Theory X-Theory Y, Benjamin Bloom's Taxonomy, and Abraham Maslow's Hierarchy of Needs. This integration makes use of existing theories to inform practical situations and helps define further the complexity and centrality of the teacher's role in a demo-cratically organized district.

Douglas McGregor published his book *The Human Side of Enterprise* in 1960. It concerns the attitude of workers toward their jobs. His studies found that Theory X individuals dislike work and therefore require authoritarian managers to make certain that they behave according to pre-established ex-pectations. Theory Y individuals naturally like work and in a satisfying job can be creative contributors who are committed to the organization. [13]

Theory Y persons are most productive working with democratic leaders. In the field of education this means that democratic leaders should begin with the assumption that all teachers are Theory Y individuals and then work to develop those who are not. Authoritarian administrators (versus democratic leaders) assume that all teachers are Theory X individuals. This assumption locks out the positive involvement of Theory Y teachers who in most schools comprise the majority. These are the teachers who enter the profession be-cause they like being with students and want to help create a better society through their professional work. A second theory that helps to clarify the important role of teachers in above-the-line functions is Benjamin Bloom's taxonomy.

Benjamin Bloom developed a classification of learning levels in 1956. This is usually pictured as a pyramid beginning at the bottom with informa-tion/knowledge gathering and progressing through comprehension, applica-tion, analysis, synthesis, and ending at the top with evaluation. Student learn-ing is often directed at the lowest level where it focuses on information recall. Learning concepts in depth, developing complex ideas, and creatively solving problems are actions that happen at progressively higher steps. Long-lasting learning occurs at the analysis, synthesis, and evaluation levels. [14]

For learning situations to be most fulfilling, it is important for both stu-dents and teachers to progress through all levels of the taxonomy. The pyra-mid is a helpful image indicating that each step should build on the one beneath it. While it is possible for learning to occur at the top without the bottom foundation, this is not desirable as it often results in opinions being given without hard information for support. A graphic representation of Bloom's taxonomy is shown in figure 2.4.

A practical example may be helpful in understanding the different levels of this taxonomy. Let us consider a high school history lesson on the American Revolution. Many teachers stress the knowledge/information level by having students memorize chronological charts of events such as the Proclamation of 1763, the Stamp Act of 1765, the Townshend Acts of 1767, and so on.

Dates of these events and their significance are often forgotten within a relatively short period of time. Students seldom move to analysis or synthesis levels where they might compare the characteristics of the American Revolu-

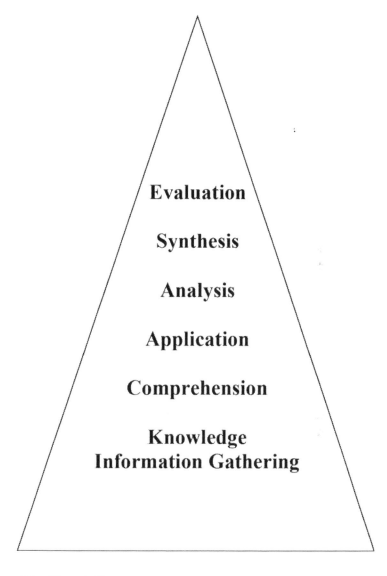

Evaluation

Synthesis

Analysis

Application

Comprehension

Knowledge
Information Gathering

Figure 2.4.   Bloom's Taxonomy

tion to the revolutions in France and Russia. When they have done this, they then can begin to evaluate whether the American Revolution was a revolution, a war for independence, or merely a side accompaniment to the larger world struggle between France and Great Britain. This synthesis will be long remembered.

A third theory that helps to understand the complex role of the teacher in a democratically organized school district is Abraham Maslow's hierarchy of needs. Maslow's *Motivation and Personality* was originally published in 1954 and modified in 1970. His original five-stage hierarchy of human needs is graphically pictured as a pyramid beginning with physical needs at the bottom followed by security/safety, belongingness/love, esteem, and self-actualization. In a pyramid one usually cannot move to a higher step unless those beneath it are satisfied.[15] A graphic pyramid representation of Maslow's hierarchy is shown in figure 2.5.

The ideal situation for an individual as well as the school is to exist at the self-actualization level as often as possible. Teachers at this level are those who are willing to do almost anything for their students. They come to school early, stay for extra activities, work hard at home to prepare meaningful lessons, actively engage students throughout the day, spend money from their own pockets when necessary, contact parents regularly, volunteer for curriculum writing, serve on committees, and do a host of other activities that make them a principal's dream. These are teachers who truly love their profession and see themselves as part of a complex mission to affect the future well-being of society.

Effective schools have many such teachers. The goal for school leaders is to have nearly all teachers function at this level. It is the responsibility of leaders to provide environments and opportunities for this to happen. They need to recognize that each step on the pyramid needs to be fulfilled in order to reach the top.

Physical needs can be met in part by leaders ensuring that there are adequate salary schedules and fringe benefits. School environments should be safe, secure, clean, and comfortable. Principals can help ensure that all staff members feel that they are a valued part of the whole by regularly having professional meetings and organizing social functions that include everyone. Positive esteem from others as well as self-esteem can be developed through transparent and proficient staff evaluations that are connected with comprehensive professional growth plans and activities.

These are some of the conditions necessary for teachers to be self-actualizing professionals. Leaders also need to recognize that many factors outside of their control can affect the teacher. A death in the family, divorce, chronic illness, loss of second income, or some other tragedy can suddenly transform a self-actualizing teacher into one who is fearful and afraid of the future.

When we integrate Maslow's pyramid with Bloom's taxonomy, McGregor's Theory X-Theory Y, and above- and below-the-line functions, a clearer picture of the important role that a teacher plays in democratically organized schools emerges. A chart of this integration would look like figure 2.6.

The ideal situation for learning in schools is to have teachers be self-actualizers (Maslow) who progress through Bloom's taxonomy and provide

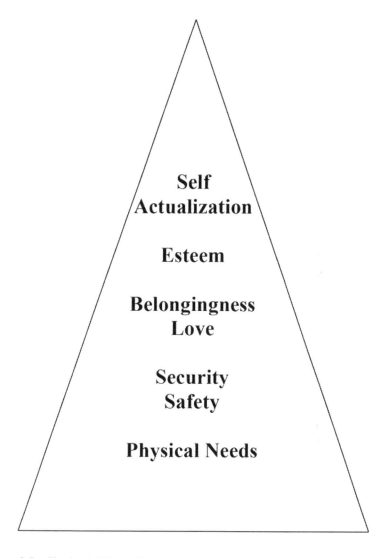

Figure 2.5. Maslow's Hierarchy

ample learning experiences for their students and themselves that emphasize analysis, synthesis, and evaluation. This situation occurs more readily when they are in a Y-oriented organization (McGregor) that encourages them to be actively involved in above-the-line activities. When teachers are denied involvement above the line and are directed to teach at the lower levels of Bloom's taxonomy, their esteem drops and they often feel insecure.

Above and Below the Line Integrated Theory

Activities	McGregor	Bloom	Maslow
• Development of mission		Evaluation	Self Actualization
• Development of policies to implement mission		Synthesis	
• Curriculum development			
• Classroom pedagogy		Analysis	Esteem
• Professional development	Y		
• Establishment of standards			
• Assessment of students			
• Budget development			
• Design of facilities			
• Community outreach			
• Development of grants		Application	
			Belongingness Love
• Implementation of policies		Compre-hension	Security/safety
• Implementation of budget			
• Implementation of security procedures			
• Implementation of support programs (transportation, food service, building maintenance)			
• Construction of master schedule	X	Knowledge/information gathering	Physical Needs
• Securing materials, supplies			

Figure 2.6.   Above- and Below-the-Line Integrated Theory

When considering the role of teachers represented by this chart relative to the demands of Federal Common Core standards as well as the testing required by individual states, it becomes clear that oftentimes teachers are seen as little more than assembly-line workers. Tests and standards are developed apart from a district and school's mission. Both curriculum and pedagogy are dictated by outside forces. Isolated tests drive learning and reduce teachers to automatons.

A far better way to create exciting learning environments is to have self-actualizing teachers working at the higher levels of Bloom's taxonomy in a democratically organized school where they are involved in above-the-line activities. It is in the intellectual space above the line that communities of learners are created. It is here that school administrators can be transformed into educational leaders. It is here that a metamorphosis can occur for their faculties as they become communities of learners.

Creating Communities of Learners by Bonding through Books

One way of creating these communities and achieving this metamorphosis is by bonding through books. Common readings and dialogues are magical ways of building communities of learners. Such experiences are important means to develop common philosophies based on both intellectual and emotional sharing. They are a way of giving teachers openings where their voices can be heard.

Richard Gibboney, former educational leadership professor at the University of Pennsylvania, believes that democratic dialogue sessions can help to improve schools. In his book *The Stone Trumpet* he wrote:

> Can something as ordinary as conversation make schools better? Can conversation between teachers and their principal informed by solid readings be a useful way to revitalize schools choking on busyness and routine? I believe there is great intellectual and practical power in a reform process that honors ideas, that respects practitioners' rich practical knowledge of education and their school, and which dignifies people in honest talk.[16]

Teachers in the Owen J. Roberts school district case study described in this chapter had been involved in numerous book-bonding experiences before the neo-Nazi crisis. These dialogue sessions were usually organized by building and used readings to focus on particular topics or suggested needs. Teachers committed to approximately nine sessions per year and were compensated by receiving either university credits or additional pay. More than four-fifths of the teachers in the district participated in this program over approximately eleven years. These dialogue experiences seemed to have empowered teachers and helps explain why they took leadership roles in confronting the neo-Nazi crisis.

Book dialogues were not the only experiences used to create communities of learners in the Owen J. Roberts school district. Teachers, principals, and other school leaders took field trips to the historic Eastern State Penitentiary;

the U.S. Holocaust Memorial Museum in Washington, DC; the Franklin Institute; the Philadelphia Museum of Art; and the Academy of Music to hear the Philadelphia Orchestra. It was the book experiences, however, that intellectually and emotionally bonded teachers and administrators. These experiences also formed the foundation for the creation of public pedagogy that emerged following the confrontation with the neo-Nazis.

PUBLIC PEDAGOGY

The role of educators in developing public pedagogy cannot be overemphasized. In a democracy they bear particular leadership responsibilities for an educated citizenry. Educators need to enter the public sphere and construct a space wherein politics and education intersect. In most cases teachers and school leaders are honored in their communities and possess the abilities needed to create conditions for effective public pedagogy.

The political world that educators enter need not be the one to which they have grown accustomed wherein citizens are manipulated by commanding pressure groups and powerful unseen individuals. Rather it could be one similar to that described by the ancient Athenian Pericles as a place wherein "a spirit of reverence [pervades] our public acts"[17] and where a person who was not involved in politics was seen "not as unambitious but as useless."[18]

Current educational theorist Henry Giroux echoes the importance that Pericles ascribed to public participation. Giroux believes that educators play a key role in preparing citizens for public participation in a democracy. He wrote that "learning must be linked not just to learning in the schools but extended to shaping public life and social relationships."[19] He described public pedagogy as a combination of education and politics in the production of meaning and social practices. He wrote in *The Mouse That Roared*, "the production of meaning, social practices, and desires—or what may be called public pedagogy—must be addressed as both an educational issue and a matter of politics and institutional power."[20]

In writing about the September 11, 2001, terrorists attacks, Giroux defined public pedagogy further: "Educators within both public schools and higher education need to continue finding ways of entering the world of politics by both making social problems visible and contesting their manifestation in the polity."[21] Such interactive processes are critical for the survival of a democracy. Timothy Stanley wrote in a special section on "Democracy and Civic Engagement" in the September 2003 issue of the *Kappan* that "democracy cannot survive unless people come together in dialogue to develop shared projects despite differences and without unduly imposing their conceptions of the good life on others."[22]

The encounter between the Pottstown SS and the Owen J. Roberts school district is a clear example of public pedagogy. Using encounters in this way is similar to taking advantage of a special teachable moment in the classroom. Michael O'Malley, an educator at Texas State University, described such events as "hinges" that can be utilized to enter students' minds and engage the public in substantive, democratic dialogue.[23] Public pedagogy can be built from such hinges if educators are willing to commit themselves to entering the domain of politics. They can be strengthened when they do so by the theories of John Dewey.

Educators can find a theoretical foundation for public pedagogy in some of Dewey's values advocated more than a century ago. These are democratic principles and include honoring the significance of each individual, recognizing the central importance that personal experiences play in an individual's continuous education, and connecting goals of social worth to educational processes. Dewey expressed these as follows:

> A society which makes provision for participation in its good of all its members on equal terms and which secures flexible readjustment of its institutions through interaction of the different forms of associated life is in so far democratic. Such a society must have a type of education which gives individuals a personal interest in social relationships and control and the habits of mind which secure social changes without introducing disorder.[24]

The public pedagogy that emerged in the Owen J. Roberts school district manifested Dewey's principles. This pedagogy grew from the dangers of the neo-Nazi threat and provided rich educational dialogue regarding hate group activities and strategies. In dialogue sessions participants were viewed as equal members of society who identified and recognized a common problem. As a result greater awareness of social relationships and enlightened civic values emerged within the community.

Another example of public pedagogy was the way in which teachers, administrators, and board members of the school district led the community in discussing some of the possible underlying causes of the Columbine massacres that occurred approximately five years after the attempted neo-Nazi boycott. These discussions centered on an important book regarding alienated youth by Patricia Hersch: *A Tribe Apart*.

COLUMBINE AND *A TRIBE APART*

Columbine—April 20, 1999—is a day etched in the minds of most Americans as one of enormous tragedy and disbelief. As a nation we knew there were problems of violence in many of our inner-city schools. These were usually ignored as they were someone else's problem. Columbine shocked the nation. It stunned complacent citizens with its raw brutality. It ended naïve beliefs that students in our affluent suburbs were safely and gratefully attending schools that were preparing them for a prosperous life.

Following Columbine, salespeople were quick to make phone calls and write e-mails to school administrators telling them of the latest surveillance equipment or trying to sell them mesh or clear plastic backpacks for students. Leaders in the Owen J. Roberts school district recognized that they needed to do more than turn the schools into tightly patrolled security islands. They took a different approach that built on the public pedagogy concept demonstrated in the neo-Nazi confrontation.

Their approach grew from statements made by then Pennsylvania Secretary of Education Eugene Hickok when he told a statewide meeting of superintendents and other administrators that if they wanted to understand the Columbine tragedy they should read Patricia Hersch's book *A Tribe Apart*. Owen J. Roberts's administrators heard his comments and asked if he would lead teachers in a discussion of the book at the opening teachers' meeting in the fall provided they read the book over the summer. He agreed, and books were provided to all of the teachers in anticipation of the meeting.

There was much excitement at that opening meeting. It was not often that the state secretary of education came into the area, and the media coverage was extensive. Hickok talked about the book in an auditorium filled with the district's teachers, administrators, board members, citizens, and media representatives. Following this session he went to several schools for more intimate meetings. These opened other wide-ranging discussions on the general themes of the book that describe the often secret lives of teenagers growing up in an affluent Washington, DC, suburb.

Following these meetings, many teachers continued to have dialogue sessions regarding the book and its implications. Some gave copies of their book to aides, cafeteria workers, secretaries, and other school employees. The dialogues eventually spread to members of the various school Parent Teacher Associations (PTAs) and other interested citizens. Many parents said that they had conversations with their children about the book. Some PTAs made plans to develop parental guidelines regarding acceptable student curfew hours, safe locations for student recreation, information regarding legal penalties for adults serving alcohol to minors, and other issues.

SUMMARY

This chapter has described a confrontation between a neo-Nazi group known as the Pottstown SS and the Owen J. Roberts school district. It has also explained the theoretical foundations for the emergence of a public pedagogy that turned the entire community into a classroom. This pedagogy grew from a series of dialogue groups that were aimed at building a common philosophy. The role of teachers as key decision makers helped to turn the confrontation into a teachable moment that became a learning opportunity for the entire community.

The key role played by teachers also manifested the progressive child-centered philosophy of John Dewey that recognizes the importance of quality education for the perpetuation of our democracy. Democracies are fragile and need to be constantly nourished by citizen participation. Public pedagogy, such as that exhibited in this case study, is one way of providing this nourishment without which our democratic ideals will surely perish. Another public pedagogy case study presented was a reaction to the violent school shootings at Columbine.

The Columbine tragedy not only provided a catalyst for development of a public pedagogy but can also be seen as a clear warning sign that something may be wrong in the very structure of our public schools. Alienated youth are found in every school district. The violent shootings in our schools did not end with Columbine. Tragically they continue to this day. The subject of chapter 3 is an examination of student alienation and the possibility that the very philosophic structure of most of our current public schools may be a contributing factor.

NOTES

1. Emmanuel Clary, "Himmler Flyer," distributed throughout Owen J. Roberts school district, April 1994.

2. Ibid.

3. Mark Schneider, "Triple Murder Causes Alarm about Hate Groups' Growth," *New York Times*, March 6, 1995.

4. Himmler Flyer.

5. Floyd Cochran, "How Hate Groups Recruit Our Young People," Newsletter of the Montana Office of Public Instruction, November/December 1992.

6. Ann Van Dyke, "So Now What Do You Do?" Pennsylvania Human Relations Council, distributed to Owen J. Roberts high school dialogue group, April 26, 1994.

7. Jim Kerr, "Riot Rumor Keeps Students Home," *Pottstown Mercury*, May 7, 1994, 1.

8. "Hate Groups State Totals," Southern Poverty Law Center, http://www.splcenter.org/intel/map/hate.jsp (accessed December 27, 2017).

9. Lawrence Cremin, *The Transformation of the School* (New York: Vintage Books Random House, 1964), 136.

10. Laurel Tanner, *Dewey's Laboratory School* (New York: Teachers College Press, 1997), 73.

11. Maxine Greene, *Teacher as Stranger* (Belmont, CA: Wadsworth Publishing Company, 1973), 7.

12. Ibid., 298.

13. For a general overview regarding Douglas McGregor's theories, the reader might want to visit https://www.toolshero.com/leadership/mcgregor-theory/ or some other readily available site.

14. For a general overview regarding Benjamin Bloom's theories, the reader might want to visit https://www.google.com/search?q=benjamin+bloom+taxonomy&oq=Benjamin+Bloom&

aqs=chrome.3.69i57j0l5.10118j0j4&sourceid=chrome&ie=UTF-8 or some other readily available site.

15. For a general overview of Abraham Maslow's theories, the reader might want to visit https://www.businessballs.com/self-awareness/maslows-hierarchy-of-needs-2026/ or some other readily available site.

16. Richard Gibboney, *The Stone Trumpet* (Albany: State University of New York Press, 1994), 205.

17. Thucydides, "Pericles' Funeral Oration," http://hrlibrary.umn.edu/education/thucydides.html (accessed January 18, 2018).

18. Ibid.

19. Henry Giroux, *Border Crossings* (New York: Routledge, Chapman, and Hall, 1992), 15.

20. Henry Giroux, *The Mouse That Roared* (New York: Rowman & Littlefield Publishers, 1999), 4.

21. Henry Giroux, "Democracy, Freedom and Justice after September 11th," http://www.tcrecord.org/content.asp?contentid=10871 (accessed January 18, 2018).

22. Timothy Stanley, "Creating the 'Space' for Civic Dialogue," *Kappan* (September 2003): 38.

23. Michael O'Malley, "Public Pedagogy and Educational Leadership: Possibilities for Critical Engagement," presentation at the Curriculum and Pedagogy Conference, Miami University, Miami, Ohio, October 6, 2005.

24. John Dewey, *Democracy and Education* (1916; New York: Macmillan Company, 1966), 99.

Chapter Three

Combating Student Alienation That Can Lead to Hatred and Violence

"Massacre at Columbine High, Bloodbath Leaves 15 Dead, 28 Hurt," *Denver Post*, April 21, 1999[1]

"'A Horrific, Horrific Day': At Least 17 Killed in Florida School Shooting," *Washington Post*, February 15, 2018[2]

"Aztec High School Shooting: 2 Slain Students Identified," *CNN* [3]

These are only three examples of the multiple school shootings by students that have occurred in the United States in recent years. The first tells of the infamous 1999 Columbine shootings that cast a national spotlight on alienated students striking back at their fellow students. The second deals with the infamous school shooting at Parkland, Florida's Marjory Stoneman Douglas High School, where another alienated student brutally used an assault rifle to mow down students at his former high school. The third example is of yet another vicious shooting where a former student of Aztec High School in Aztec, New Mexico, entered the school and killed two students who were barricaded inside an office area. The third example is not as well-known—an indication that as a nation we are becoming numb to these events.

While these are extreme examples, most schools have some alienated students. Many are isolated individuals. Some cluster together in groups that go by various names. The disappointment, resentment, and revulsion that many of them feel toward their schools usually remains bottled up inside. Sometimes, as these headlines proclaim, the alienation turns into a hatred that ends in violence. Such acts expose serious flaws both in our society and in the educational system that nourishes it.

The stories accompanying these headlines present facts and narratives that capture the depths of these calamities. They suggest that cultural or social factors may have contributed to the apparent dysfunction of the killers. What they do not do is probe in any substantive way the possibility that one of the major contributing factors may be the schools themselves.

There are many inherent imperfections in the high-stakes testing philosophy that has dominated our schools for the past several years. Beginning in the 1980s this movement reached a climax with the No Child Left Behind Act of 2001 and continues today with national and state tests dictated by federal Common Core standards. Preparation for high-stakes testing often eliminates or reduces subjects other than reading/language arts and math from the curriculum. Pressure on students is often extreme. As one fifth-grade Pennsylvania student reported to her principal when asked what her dream for the school year was, she responded, "I hope that I can just become proficient (average) this year."[4] It has ironically left many not only behind but also estranged by an educational system that was supposed to lead them into full citizenship as members of our democratic society.

This chapter briefly examines some roots of the high-stakes testing philosophy that dominates American education today. It presents a contrasting child-centered philosophy and examples from elementary, middle, and high schools where teachers and administrators made a significant difference in alleviating some of the causes of student alienation.

MODERNITY, EFFICIENCY, AND NO CHILD LEFT BEHIND

Modernity

The basic tenets of the No Child Left Behind Act and the state tests dictated by the federal Common Core standards are rooted in the modern era of the twentieth century. Frederick W. Taylor's efficiency movement imposed a high degree of standardization on many aspects of American life, including education. It was this movement that introduced us to the idea that standards and their assessments should be set by specialists. These individuals usually exert great influence over authorities near the top of a hierarchal structure that is often far removed from either production workers or—in the case of education—classroom teachers.

A basic organizational chart typical of most school districts resembles a top-down administrative structure (see figure 2.1 in chapter 2). In this model it is assumed that power flows from top to bottom. Students and parents seldom appear on such charts. If teachers are included they are usually at the bottom, where they receive directives from above. A similar organizational chart in action can be seen in a satire of the efficiency movement created by Charlie Chaplin in his classic 1936 movie *Modern Times*.

Modern Times

Charlie Chaplin wrote, directed, and starred in *Modern Times*, a film that presents a stinging indictment of an assembly line in which the efficiency movement has turned the workers into automatons trapped by the forces of a technological society gone awry. Chaplin is a helpless individual deeply affected by the actions of a heartless bureaucracy whose only concern is bottom-line profits.

His job as a worker on an assembly line at the Electro Steel Company is to tighten screws on some imaginary product. He does this until he becomes dazed from the monotonous repetition and is granted permission to punch out on the time clock in order to take a break. While in the restroom, he lights a cigarette and begins to unwind. The relaxation is short lived as the corporate boss suddenly appears on a wall-sized TV monitor and orders him back to work.

The boss controls all aspects of the company's operations while at ease in his comfortable office. He lackadaisically reads comics from a newspaper, arranges pieces of a puzzle, and occasionally gives orders to his secretary. His main function appears to be observing the efficiency of all assembly-line jobs. Periodically he orders the line supervisor to speed up Charlie's line. This causes Charlie to fall behind. Fellow workers become angry. He eventually cracks under the strain, falls into a trancelike state, and becomes caught between phantasmagorical motorized gears.[5]

The issues of power and control portrayed in this scene are enormous. Workers had no voice in decisions affecting the quality of their products or other aspects of their jobs. Efficiency experts, pictured in one scene attempting to modernize the lunch break through a mechanical feeding machine, made decisions that were enforced by commanding authorities. The workers had no stake in the organization other than their paychecks. In most respects they were captives of a system wherein they were isolated and controlled by a powerful force they seldom saw. In many respects their factory resembled the panopticon prisons described by the French philosopher Michel Foucault in his book *Discipline and Punish*. In such a prison, inmates were controlled by a powerful central tower where a faceless power unknown to them directed all aspects of their lives.

Charlie's factory differed from a panopticon prison in one major aspect. The prison existed strictly to control individuals. The factory controlled individuals in order to manufacture products. The ends of the prison became the means of the factory. In such an environment, the workers were invested in the finished product only as far as their specific task was concerned. It is assumed from the movie that each assembly line added small contributions until the product was completed. At this point in the manufacturing process it is common for trained inspectors to sort, examine, and measure the products. If within established tolerances, they are sent out into the world. If not, they are recycled or discarded. Comparisons can be readily made between an assembly-line process, such as the one created on film by Charlie Chaplin, and many American schools today.

Students as Products

The No Child Left Behind Act of 2001 and subsequent state tests and standards such as the federal Common Core treat students as products that are regularly sorted, examined, and measured through a system of high-stakes tests. Though they may differ from state to state, their purpose is the same: assess students regularly to determine if they, the teacher, and the school have made yearly progress. The testing pressure on students is enormous. Failure to meet test standards can mean that students will be recycled through after-school or summertime remediation programs. Many of these students, especially in high school, will be discarded altogether.

The pressure on teachers and building principals, particularly at the elementary level, is also huge. They know that if their class or building does not reach targeted annual goals, they stand the risk of being transferred or losing their jobs.[6] In this high-anxiety environment they often ignore the mandated curriculum and focus on the subjects that will be tested—reading, language arts, and math. The tests dictate the curriculum.

One example of this deference to high-stakes tests is seen in Philadelphia where thirteen fifth- and sixth-grade teachers received an e-mail from an assistant principal instructing them to stop teaching the state-mandated social studies curriculum from December through April. The time scheduled for social studies was to be used for math instead. Math was considered of vital importance because of the impending exams in April. Social studies was not a subject tested for annual progress.[7] Another example is found in a suburban Philadelphia school district where a superintendent ordered principals to stop teaching elementary science and social studies altogether and concentrate instead on reading, language arts, and math.[8]

As with the workers on the assembly line in Charlie's factory, mandated tests focus on narrow tasks. There is an assumption that somehow, someplace, someone else is responsible for the final product. Social studies, a subject that includes topics concerned with citizenship preparation, will only be measured later by the quality of a person's participation in a democratic society. Sadly, many will not participate at all.

A common philosophy regarding power relationships and the value of individuals unites the assembly-line factory depicted by Chaplin and a school driven by high-stakes tests. It is found in John Locke's seventeenth-century views of a child at birth.

John Locke's "White Paper"

John Locke was an immensely significant seventeenth-century philosopher who greatly influenced the formation of our nation. His *Second Treatise of Government* was read widely by many of the founding fathers. His basic concepts regarding the intrinsic rights of individuals versus the authority of a monarchy inspired Thomas Jefferson and others to write the Declaration of Independence. In this same treatise, Locke presents arguments for the sanctity of private property, a limitation on the authority of central government, and a separation of power between legislative and executive functions.

Locke was also an educational philosopher. His ideas concerning the nature of a child at birth are as influential in American culture today as are his political thoughts. He believed that a child at birth was "white paper, void of all characters, without any ideas."[9] This *tabula rasa* or blank slate philosophy places vast authority and responsibility for a person's education in the hands of parents and teachers. Inherent in such authority and responsibility is the power to control the individual until he or she reaches a majority age, identified by Locke in *The Second Treatise* as twenty-one.

Locke's white paper philosophy denies the innate qualities of a child at birth. If the opposite is true—if a child at birth has intrinsic capacities, passions, and talents—then the notion of total control by those in authority needs to be modified. The implications of this change for education are enormous. They place the student in the center rather than at the bottom of a system's organizational chart.

AN ALTERNATIVE PHILOSOPHY

Placing the Student in the Center

As pictured previously, an organizational chart dominated by efficiency concerns and based on a *tabula rasa* philosophy of a child at birth places the student at the bottom. An alternative philosophy, one that places the child at the center of the educational process, resembles a series of circles as shown in figure 2.2 in chapter 2.

Placing the student at the center of the process dramatically shifts relationships. This presents a different way of considering power that flows both from students and to students. The importance of considering the unique gifts that students bring to their educational experience is emphasized in this visualization. An effective way of thinking about the importance of each position relative to the daily education of a student is to consider the amount of intended education that takes place if each individual on the chart is unexpectedly absent from school.

If the student is absent, little designated education will take place. If the teacher is absent, there may be some education provided there is a skilled substitute. If a support staff member (secretary, aide, bus driver, custodian, cafeteria worker) misses a day, the class will continue to function fairly normally. If the principal is absent, few will notice. If the superintendent or another central office staff member misses a day, hardly anyone will notice. School board members, as well as state and federal officials, seldom visit schools during the day and are not usually well known by teachers and students.

The educational philosophy supporting placing the child in the center of the educational hierarchy comes from another famous political theorist who is also prominent as an educational philosopher: Jean Jacques Rousseau.

Jean Jacques Rousseau and a "Cathedral Within"

Jean Jacques Rousseau is one of France's revolutionary heroes. His stinging anti-establishment works made him a venerated philosopher of the 1789 revolution. Consider one example: he begins Book One of *On the Social Contract* with words that have inspired not only French but other revolutionaries as well: "Man is born free and everywhere he is in chains."[10]

Rousseau's views on education are similarly radical and differ dramatically from Locke's *tabula rasa*. His *Discourse on the Arts and Sciences*, written in 1750, was the winning entry to an essay contest question regarding whether the advancement of the arts and sciences had improved morals. He answered strongly that it had not. This essay argued in effect that education can corrupt the beauty of an individual at birth. He wrote in his book on education, *Emile*, that "everything is good as it leaves the hands of the Author of things; everything degenerates in the hands of man."[11]

An effective metaphor that captures Rousseau's view of a child at birth is provided by Norman Cousins, the former editor of the *Saturday Review* magazine. Cousins interviewed many of the world's most influential people and often asked them to describe the most important thing they had learned in their lifetime. One of these was the 1952 Nobel Peace Prize recipient, Albert Schweitzer. Talented as a writer, musician, scientist, and doctor, he could have lived a comfortable life. He chose a different path and established medical clinics where none existed in the tropics of Africa.

Cousins traveled far into a jungle to interview Schweitzer and during a meal one evening asked his question. Schweitzer said that he would have to think about his response and would have an answer the following day. The next morning Cousins awoke to find that Schweitzer had gone into a neighboring village to help deliver a baby. After his return that evening, Schweitzer told Cousins he had thought about the question throughout the day and saw his answer in the newborn infant. He believed that the most important thing he had learned in his lifetime was that each person contains a "cathedral within."[12]

Schweitzer's metaphor, captured by Cousins, is of a vast, beautiful, sacred newborn. It is consistent with Rousseau's philosophy and creates a tense dialectic with John Locke's white paper image. It is this dialectic that America's most famous educational philosopher, John Dewey, attempted to resolve through his theories that consistently place the child in the center of the educational process.

John Dewey and the Significance of Placing the Child in the Center of the Educational Process

John Dewey wrestled with Locke's and Rousseau's educational theories and attempted to resolve them.[13] In doing so he leaned more toward Rousseau's view and placed the child in the center of the educational process. This was a radical departure in American education when it was presented more than one hundred years ago. It continues to create significant tensions as it confronts the dominant child-control theory, evident in the high-stakes testing movement that drives American education today. The following quotation from Dewey's *The School and the Society, the Child and the Curriculum* captures the heart of his philosophy:

> The child is the starting-point, the center, and the end. His development, his growth, is the ideal. It alone furnishes the standard. To the growth of the child all studies are subservient; they are instruments valued as they serve the needs of growth. Personality, character, is more than subject-matter. Not knowledge or information, but self-realization, is the goal. To possess all the world of knowledge and lose one's own self is as awful a fate in education as in religion. Moreover, subject-matter never can be got into the child from without. Learning is active. It involves reaching out of the mind. It involves organic assimilation starting from within.[14]

The Progressive philosophy summarized by this quotation challenges the very basis of an educational system that imposes a curriculum dictated by high-stakes tests on students. It recognizes that true learning starts from within each individual and can lead to unique self-actualization. Dewey does not stop here. He believed further that the individual is situated within a democratic social context and that developing values of social worth are a critical component of each student's education.[15]

The significance of these beliefs cannot be overemphasized. It is in this philosophy that the possibilities of confronting hatred that often grow out of student alienation lie. Many school leaders on all levels—teachers, principals, superintendents—have applied the core aspects of Dewey's philosophy in specific situations and have made a difference in student's lives.

THEORY TO PRACTICE: CONFRONTING ALIENATION BEFORE IT TURNS INTO HATRED OR VIOLENCE

Meade Elementary School

Located on North 18th Street, General George C. Meade Elementary School is in one of the most economically disadvantaged areas of Philadelphia. From a distance Meade is an imposing structure. The school was built in 1936 when urban schools were still the pride of their neighborhoods. These were the places where recent migrants' dreams of the future could become realities. As temples of learning, they were not cheap structures. Expensive materials such as marble, terrazzo, and brass were used freely.

Today a fence separates the school from the broken bottles, street trash, and dangers that litter the neighborhood. When approaching the school you wonder if you really want to go inside. Then, passing through the gate, something magical happens. Here you walk into a beautiful garden and arboretum that are a cooperative project between the school and a suburban Rotary Club. The main entrance invites you in through large doors with highly shined brass fixtures. [16]

The welcoming atmosphere continues inside the main lobby. Rocking chairs, live plants, fish aquaria, and carts containing books await students, parents, and visitors. Walking through the lobby into the main hallway, you enter a mysterious world in which students have filled the walls and ceilings with artwork to simulate a tropical rainforest. Hallways on all three floors proudly display student work. The top floor of the school, in what had been an unused corner, contains a Japanese garden constructed by the school's computer teacher.

Classrooms are filled with learning centers, books, and student work proudly displayed everywhere. Students and teachers are actively engaged in real learning. One classroom in particular stands out. This is a reading recovery room where students experiencing serious reading problems go for special help. The soothing sounds of classical music playing in the background create a counterpoint to a carpeted room that is alive with books and artwork. A plate of cookies waits on a table for hungry children to help themselves. A very special teacher and her volunteer mother patiently teach children about the mysterious and wonderful worlds that await them in books.

This school is truly an oasis, a life-giving center, for a depressed neighborhood. Many failing Philadelphia schools have been taken over by outsider managers or reconstituted by the district because of low achievement. This is not true of Meade. In fact the school exceeds expectations on district-wide standardized tests and has been allowed to keep many of its unique arrangements while other schools in the district have been forced to standardize their practices based on centralized models. This school operates on democratic principles that give power for many decisions to the teachers most affected by those decisions.

An example of a democratic principle at work is the reduction in class size for the primary grades. Under principal Frank Murphy's guidance, teachers voted on how to best use funds designated for intervention programs aimed at failing students. Rather than follow the traditional model of hiring student-specific tutors that pulled students from classrooms, they decided to add an additional teacher so as to reduce class sizes for all primary students.

The success of this school can be attributed to dedicated, involved teachers led by the school principal Frank Murphy.[17] Several years ago Murphy began engaging his staff in multiple dialogue sessions aimed at improving the school. Teams designed curricula, set budget priorities, focused on problem students, and worked with parents and the surrounding community to make the school a center for the neighborhood.

Murphy reached out wherever he could to support these teachers and bring needed resources to the school. Soon after becoming the principal in 1997, he contacted the Philadelphia Writing Project and inquired about becoming involved in a sustained venture to develop literacy skills among his students. This led to development of a nationally recognized program. Mary Ann Smith, director of governmental relations and public affairs for the National Writing Project, praised Murphy and his staff for "giving students access to the world through literacy."[18]

Another of Murphy's innovations was the development of a partnership with Temple University in Philadelphia. Among the many benefits from this partnership is a project that brings after-school music opportunities to students. Here they are not only exposed to a variety of musical activities but also can learn to play an assortment of instruments.

These examples demonstrate ways that Frank Murphy and his teachers respected the cathedral that they find in each child. David Warner, former editor of *Philadelphia City Paper*, visited Meade as part of a Principal for a Day program. He praised the learning that he found as well as the positive attitudes of the principal, teachers, and students. He summarized his visit by writing, "If you treat the students with respect, respect is what you get back. If you treat them as test-takers and stuff them into inadequate facilities, a failing school is what you get back."[19]

Meade Elementary is an example of a school where the principal and teachers worked closely with students and parents to achieve success against great obstacles. Theirs was a community effort that manifests the philosophy of John Dewey. They truly did practice his beliefs by placing the well-being of each child in the center of the educational hierarchy. Alienation resulting from learning imposed from outside the child was not an option. At Meade students did not hate school but welcomed its loving embrace.

Whereas Meade is an example of an entire school manifesting Dewey's child-centered philosophy, the next case illustrates ways a single teacher within a school developed a program aimed at preventing failure, alienation, and hatred among primary-aged students.

A Primary Teacher's Unique Reading Program

It is revealing, perhaps even shocking, to examine the school records of high school students who are labeled as potential failures or dropouts. More often than not their problems began in the early primary grades and are usually associated with the acquisition of reading and language arts skills. A primary teacher named Ellen Keys in a rural/suburban district called Midview located outside of Cleveland, Ohio, recognized this fact. She knew that if students experienced failure in the early grades they not only rejected themselves but also became alienated from the system that imposed the failure on them. She had a better idea and worked hard to provide a learning environment in which all students succeeded.

Fighting against a system that dictated a common reading program for all students, Ellen developed an alternative and convinced her principal to initiate an experimental program in her school. Approximately fifteen kindergarten students who were not ready for a phonics-based first-grade reading curriculum were identified. With the consent of their parents, they were placed in a transitional first grade in which a unique approach to reading gave them a real chance at success.

Ellen sought aides from several senior citizen volunteers to help her with the program. This was an excellent move as it brought seniors into contact with students whose own grandparents were often absent. It also provided the seniors important contacts with youngsters that were often missing in their lives.

These aides were needed as the reading/language arts program was intensely personal. One particularly interesting activity demonstrates the philosophy used by Ellen. She gave each student a prompt, often regarding animals or pets, and asked him or her to tell her a brief story about it. Ellen recorded the students' responses and, working with them over several days, showed them how their spoken words looked when turned into written words. The words were placed at the bottom of pages until they resembled a picture book minus the pictures. She then arranged with the high school art teacher to have several of his students illustrate the stories.

Once all the books were illustrated, Ellen organized a luncheon in her classroom that brought together the high school illustrators with the first-grade authors. The menu was simple: vegetable soup prepared by the senior citizens. The atmosphere in the classroom was anything but simple. Both authors and illustrators beamed with warm pride and joy on meeting each other. Bridging generations by bringing together senior citizens, high school students, and first graders through reading and language arts benefited everyone.

Following the luncheon, each of the books was laminated and put into the school library. Parents and their children were invited in for an evening conference to review student progress. This can be a tense time for teachers, parents, and students. Not this time. As part of the conference students proudly took their parents into the library and showed them their books.

Rather than hating books and the reading and writing associated with them, these students discovered the joy that can come from investing themselves in a creative project. It is not possible to say that Ellen Keys prevented failures later in these students' school careers. It is also not possible to say that she kept them from feeling alienated from school or the greater society as they grew older. It is possible to say that in this instance she gave them a chance at success, and most of them responded favorably. Ellen may not have known that she was following a philosophy similar to that advocated by John Dewey. She instinctively did know that every child mattered and that each student deserved a personalized education that placed him or her at the center of the process.[20]

Ellen Keys's classroom represents an example of a single teacher working within a system to make a difference in primary-aged children's lives. The next example illustrates ways that two middle school teachers teamed together to create an unusual program that opened doors for many students who would normally be excluded from such innovative learning opportunities.

Stream Watch: The Way It Should Be

Oftentimes the most engaging and creative programs in our schools are reserved for gifted or academically talented students. Active field experiences, self-directed learning, and engaging experimentation—attributes of many of these programs—are usually reserved for students whose IQ scores or past grades have placed them into special classes taught by the best and most creative teachers. An unusual middle school program in a rural/suburban Philadelphia school broke the admission barriers for students to enroll in such programs and opened applications for all students. The name of the program was Stream Watch. It proved to be so successful that more than 120 students applied for forty-four spaces, and students were chosen by lottery.

Stream Watch was the brainchild of two middle school teachers, David Jarvie and Tamie Fox, who had a strong interest in placing science education in the center of their sixth- and seventh-grade curriculum. Many of their activities were field based, which led to the name Stream Watch. Their pedagogy was child centered and involved active learning that connected with the world outside of the school. As David Jarvie explained it,

> Removing the walls of the classroom was very important to us. Connecting with the outside world and the individuals who were out there making a difference gave the children an opportunity to connect their learning with the real world.[21]

The traditional subjects of reading, writing, and math—usually stressed at the expense of other subjects in today's high-stakes testing environment—were included in their science activities that often integrated geology, biology, chemistry, and meteorology. The program's curriculum revolved around two themes: unity and change. Unity considered the ecological importance of a particular area, and change studied the basic physical elements of watersheds and the environmental impact modern technology has on them. Technical science support was often provided by experts from a regional natural sciences academy.

Through these themes students explored all subjects. Social studies, for example, received special attention as students studied early Native American history, exploration, wars, and geographic factors that dictate regional economics. As David Jarvie explained, "I still smile today when I think back to the student who would, with a puzzled look on his or her face, say 'I am not sure if this is social studies or science or if this is science or math.'"[22]

The program was highly individualized and stressed independent as well as cooperative learning. Students went into depth on projects and were not constrained from doing so by bells ringing to tell them it was time to switch from one subject to another. They became responsible for their own learning and often graded themselves by developing portfolios using rigorous rubrics created by the teachers. Written narratives of student progress were shared weekly with parents. Students planned their own open houses and other ways of reporting their progress to parents and the community.

One interesting aspect of the program was that it grouped sixth- and seventh-graders together into a class of approximately forty-four students. They stayed together for two years and developed a strong sense of community as well as self-discipline. Seventh-graders took on leadership roles for the sixth-graders. They taught them the science protocols and served as mentors and guides. The power of peer teaching and learning was highly visible.

The Stream Watch program involved extensive community outreach. This led to many unique experiences for students. Some of these included opportunities to meet and hear renowned primatologist Jane Goodall speak about her adventures, climb Neversink Mountain and learn about the history of its trail and railroad, help sail a tall ship on the Delaware River while studying the port of Philadelphia, and meet regularly with prominent environmental scientists.

Students took great pride in the fact that they were part of Stream Watch. One of the reasons for this may have been the positive publicity that the program received from local media. Another may have been the fact that for many of the students it was a unique experience often available only in upper-level groupings.

For most of the students, this experience with independent, student-centered learning freed them to realize greater success than a more traditional text or teacher-centered course. Students who may have been alienated by a conventional educational system were connected and motivated as part of the egalitarian community that they created. The bond between Stream Watch students and their teachers was very strong. Students learned that caring teachers were part of a system that was working for and not against them.

Many students, labeled as potential dropouts, learned a similar lesson in a large suburban high school outside of Cleveland, Ohio. Here, during the early 1970s when both student activism and hostility were often a dominant element in high schools, a dynamic teacher worked to create an innovative communications program aimed specifically at reducing alienation felt by many potential dropouts.

Education through Inquiry

Tom Asad was known as the most creative teacher at Normandy High School in Parma, Ohio. He was an English teacher dedicated to making educational experiences come alive for students who hated school. For example, in teaching William Golding's *Lord of the Flies*, he took students on a weekend field trip into a wilderness area so that they could experience firsthand some of the stresses similar to Golding's school boys who were stranded on a deserted island. When teaching poetry he often took students into a candlelit room and gave them quill pens, ink, and fine vellum paper so that they could feel the beauty of words coming from inside them. He simulated some aspects of Big Brother's ever-present surveillance as depicted in George Orwell's *Nineteen Eighty-Four* by having some students spend a night isolated in a TV studio with a camera recording all of their actions.

Tom's activities were often controversial. Normandy was a large high school with, at this time, approximately 2,700 students and 135 teachers. The day that he asked all of his students to demand their IQ scores—scores usually kept secret from students—was one of those times. Counselors were unaware of his demands and when the students began lining up outside their offices they freaked out. His reputation for both creativity and unusual actions spread into the community. One day a member of the John Birch Society was found in an adjoining classroom secretly recording one of his lessons, presumably hoping to find something damaging enough to get him fired. Even though there were complaints, he was not fired because his actions on behalf of students brought him great respect. Nowhere was this truer than with the Education through Inquiry (ETI) Program.

ETI was a program that was team taught by an English and a social studies teacher at each high school grade to approximately forty students who were labeled as potential dropouts. These were students who were considered of average ability. They were also students who had difficulty in acquiring reading and writing skills that could, in most cases, be traced back to their first years in elementary school. Because they had experienced failure in these basic areas, they hated school, were often truant, and, when in school, were generally discipline problems.

The philosophy behind ETI was simple. No society could afford to lose this type of student. A different way of learning needed to be found for them. ETI teachers, led by Tom Asad, found many alternative methods. These were usually experienced based and of great interest to students. The teachers referred to this as inductive learning. It involved many field trips, more than twenty per year, as it connected with people in real-life experiences. It also involved deeper connections with targeted members of the community. An example was a unit on drama in which students became involved with members of local community theaters and studied all aspects of play production. They then set up their own theater organizations in the classroom that led to productions for themselves as well as for other students and teachers in the school.

Another unit of interest dealt with developing expository writing skills through budgeting and meal preparation. ETI students in groups of four or five were given a set budget and had to buy food, prepare a meal in the home economics lab, and serve the food to their classmates. Students had to write out the menus, recipes, and directions in detail. Long before the idea become popular in Iron Chef competitions, they used the technique of having outsiders, often other teachers in the school, judge the quality of their meals.

Tom Asad left Normandy High School and eventually pursued a career as a writer while also teaching in California prisons. Although he has written several books, his most important contributions may well be his years teaching potential dropouts, students who hated school, that they were valued as individuals who did contain a cathedral within. His pedagogy was certainly consistent with the philosophy of John Dewey as he regularly placed students in the center of the power circles and worked hard to make learning important for them. By doing this, he eliminated some of the alienation that many felt toward school and society. A testament to the respect and love that students felt toward him was when he was chosen by a graduating class to be their commencement speaker. The applause was thunderous.

Tom Asad is only one example of teachers at Normandy High School who worked hard to bring positive educational experiences to students. Normandy was a place where education was more than a bubble sheet and students were more than statistics. The tone for the school was set by enlightened administrators. Among the best anywhere was the assistant principal, Marty Kane, who was deeply committed to reducing some of the anger and alienation that many students felt toward their school and society in general.[23]

A High School Breakfast Club and Weekend Rides with Police

A dynamic assistant principal name Marty Kane created an unusual high school breakfast club to deal with the anger and alienation experienced by some Normandy High School students. In the early 1970s many students were riding the wave of the American counterculture revolution. Normandy was a relatively new high school in Cleveland's largest suburb, Parma. It was a community of middle-class values with strong Eastern European roots and a variety of income levels.

Students represented a range of academic abilities and, as in many similar schools, there was a group of alienated students who were potential dropouts. They were seen as troublemakers and often had problems with drugs or alcohol. The school's administration consisted of a principal and assistant principal. This seems light by today's standards. Not true in this case. The special personalities and dedication of these two made them real heavyweights by any measure.

Marty worked closely with most student groups in the school. He remarkably learned most of the student's names by studying a number of yearbook pictures in the evening and then finding the students and chatting with them at school the next day. One of his main functions was to deal with potential problems before they became serious crises. One technique that he developed was a breakfast club that included what he called his top thirty students—ten from each class. When students would leave the group for whatever reason, they were replaced by others so that there was always a community of thirty.

He provided breakfast for the top thirty weekly during the school year. At these meetings they talked about school issues, situations ready to erupt, and oftentimes individual difficulties. He tried to see many of these students daily and would talk with them about their progress in school as well as personal problems. If absent from school, the student would often receive a phone call at home.

Oftentimes Marty would learn from breakfast club members about impending problems regarding other students in the school. Several episodes involved planned drinking parties at homes when parents were out of town. These tips led him to develop a close relationship with the city's police, and he would often ride with patrolmen to target destinations to stop potential tragedies. In most cases crises were avoided, and after stern warnings the parties either broke up or never occurred at all.

The breakfast club became an inspiration for other programs such as an alternative to traditional school suspensions. Suspension from school is often controversial. It may help the school environment by removing problem students but often does nothing to help the suspended student. Marty developed an alternative program that included day-long sessions for suspended students at a nearby retreat center. For example, all smoking suspensions were held on a certain date at the center. At this time counselors and health experts would work with students individually or in small groups to explore the reasons for smoking and stressing its health dangers. Students suspended for fighting might have sessions on personal anxiety, violence, and related issues.

How many disasters Marty was able to stop through these strategies is impossible to tell. What was observable was the intense loyalty that members of the breakfast club and other alienated students had for him. Theirs was not a community of losers but of winners. He worked hard to combat alienation and the hatred and violence that can grow from it.

Other students in the school held deep respect for him as well. At a time when most institutional values and the people supporting them were being questioned by youths, he stood out as a person who cared deeply about students and their education. These feelings extended to the teachers. They knew he valued each of them as much as he valued each student. His actions placed students at the center of the power circles. He inspired teachers to do the same.

The school became known for its innovations. Although it was not articulated that it was based on John Dewey's progressive philosophy, it clearly was. Actions spoke louder than words, and in this case practice informs theory. This author was one of the teachers from this school and later became a superintendent in a suburban Philadelphia school district where some of the lessons learned at Normandy High School were put into practice. [24]

Reducing Alienation through a "Motorhead" Club

As seen in the previous description, almost every high school has a group of students who feel alienated by school. For various reasons they do not quite fit in. They seem to learn best apart from traditional classrooms in which desks are in neat rows and questions and answers are in neat boxes. They are often viewed by others as misfits—the ones who, when absent, no one really misses. In many respects the system gives up and simply warehouses them until they either quit school or graduate near the bottom of the class. They go by names such as "druggies," "goths," "skaters," or "punks." In a school district near Philadelphia they were known as "Motorheads." Soon after arriving as the new superintendent in the Owen J. Roberts school district, I decided to reach out to them in hopes that their alienation would not turn into hatred and violence.

The superintendent's office overlooked the high school parking lot. From this vantage point it was possible to see a lineup of beautifully reconditioned cars that were parked in a section reserved, through unwritten rules, for the Motorheads. These students were usually the first ones to leave school and generally raced out of the parking lot while lighting up a much-craved cigarette.

A speed bump near the entrance to the superintendent's office slowed the traffic, and one day I went out and stopped the first car, a shiny yellow 1971 Plymouth, as it slowed over the bump. I identified myself to the driver, a young man of about seventeen who quickly shoved a cigarette up his sleeve. After explaining my interest in his car, I asked if he would show me the engine the next day at about the same time. Startled and relieved, the driver said he would.

The next day the student proudly raised the hood to show a modified engine that was better than showroom clean. A group of approximately twenty other Motorheads (mostly male but many accompanied by their female friends) were there as well. They began a conversation about cars—and about school. These students said that they had a tough time sitting in classes. They considered them unimportant. They found most lectures to be dull. They often slept in class.

A famous John Dewey quotation came to mind: "What the best and wisest parent wants for his own child, that must the community want for all of its children."[25] Field trips, exciting speakers, and experience-based learning were not usually available for these students. The system dictated the what, when, and how of their learning.

That afternoon things began to change. Asked if they would be interested in coming together periodically to learn through field trips and other hands-on experiences, the students responded enthusiastically. This was the beginning of the Motorhead Club that included approximately thirty members and lasted for several years.

Over the years the club did many interesting things together. One of the first, as might be expected, was to attend a car race. Members also experienced academics in different ways. One of these involved learning about Iraq and the birth of civilization by visiting a distinguished linguist at the University of Pennsylvania's Museum of Archaeology and Anthropology.

This rare scholar was compiling a dictionary of ancient Sumerian words from the vast collection of cuneiform tablets in the museum's archives. These tablets are not normally open to the public. Being familiar with the collection, I called the director and arranged a visit for a group of high school students. They were not identified as Motorheads.

In preparation for the field trip, the students met for several sessions during which they learned about the geography of Iraq, viewed portions of *Legacy: The Origins of Civilization* regarding ancient Mesopotamia, and tasted Middle Eastern food. Arrangements were made for a school bus to take them into the city and for lunch following the museum visit. There were no costs to the students—the trip was paid for from a special superintendent salary giveback fund. No special instructions were given regarding dress for the trip, and it was a pleasant surprise when the students arrived with men wearing ties and women in dresses.

When the Motorheads arrived at the museum, Dr. Erle Leichty, director of the Sumerian dictionary project, took them into a workroom containing a large number of cabinets and files. It was here that students learned about the land of Eden in present-day Iraq and the epic of Gilgamesh. The five-thousand-year-old Gilgamesh legend is of a hero-wanderer who sought eternal life. He found the plant that would give it to him at the bottom of the sea, only to have it stolen by a serpent. Gilgamesh learned the lesson that eternal life is not found on this earth.

Members of the Motorhead Club were able to hold some of the ancient tablets in their hands. As students were passing tablets from hand to hand, Dr. Leichty said that one of the largest (approximately dinner plate size), then being held by the leader of the club, was the centerpiece of the collection. The student asked what it was and learned that this was the earliest written record of the flood story—Noah's ark. This was an awestruck Hollywood moment reminiscent of *Raiders of the Lost Ark*. Imagine, a forgotten Motorhead from an average school district holding a historical artifact of immeasurable value in his grease-stained hands. Lightning bolts, indeed. On this day these students learned about history by experiencing something very deep and profoundly real. Few would soon forget this encounter with the past.

The club experienced many other learning activities that had an impact on them. One involved a visit to the New Jersey shore to go on a whale-watching adventure. This activity was motivated by a student who hated school and loved to spend time at the shore. He planned the trip and in preparation for it the Motorheads read and discussed Ernest Hemingway's *The Old Man and the Sea*. Though they did not see any whales on their voyage, they did see many other types of fish and experienced a few hours of life on the sea.

Years later this author received a letter from the young man who planned the trip. After barely graduating from high school, he went to Florida to pursue life on the beach. He later enrolled in a community college and eventually turned those years there into a four-year degree. His degree was in elementary education.

Other Motorheads wrote letters as well. Some told of going into various branches of the military or shared news of becoming parents. It is possible, maybe even probable, that many of the Motorheads may have survived school and become productive citizens without the intervention of the club. It is also possible that an elementary teacher in Florida and a sailor on board an American ship at sea may not have. America would have been the poorer for the loss. The time, effort, and money were worth the gamble.

SUMMARY

This chapter has examined some roots of the current high-stakes testing theories that dominate our nation's schools, often leading to student alienation. It has also presented a contrasting child-centered educational philosophy. This philosophy has been illuminated with concrete examples in which teachers and administrators made a difference in students' lives. We will never know if their actions helped to avoid school tragedies such as those that occurred in Colorado, Florida, or New Mexico. We do know that they enriched students' learning and lessened the alienation that many felt toward their schools.

One of the most serious and enduring threats to American democratic ideals has been hatred growing from racism. From the beginnings of our republic until today, racism has been a source of ongoing hatred that has often turned into violence. At times this hatred and violence have threatened to undermine the very existence of our democracy. The following chapter considers racism and ways that educators have dealt with it. A scholar-practitioner section that considers deconstruction and critical pedagogy helps to provide theoretical grounding for educational leaders as they combat racism.

NOTES

1. Mark Obmascik, "Massacre at Columbine High, Bloodbath Leaves 15 Dead, 28 Hurt," *Denver Post*, April 21, 1999, http://extras.denverpost.com/news/shot0420a.htm (accessed January 4, 2018).

2. Lori Rozsa, Moriah Balingit, William Wan, and Mark Berman, "'A Horrific, Horrific Day': At Least 17 Killed in Florida School Shooting," *Washington Post*, February 15, 2018 (accessed February 23, 2018).

3. Ralph Ellis, Eric Levenson, and Andrea Diaz, "Aztec High School Shooting: 2 Slain Students Identified," *CNN*, December 8, 2017, http://www.cnn.com/2017/12/07/us/aztec-high-school-shooting-new-mexico/index.html (accessed January 4, 2018).

4. Comments shared with the author by an elementary school principal during a 2015 educational leadership class at Saint Joseph's University.

5. *Modern Times*, written and directed by Charlie Chaplin (United States: United Artists, 1936).

6. The author knows of several situations in the Philadelphia school district as well as suburban districts in which teachers have been transferred and principals have lost their jobs because of a failure to meet annual testing goals.

7. Freeden Oeurr, e-mail message to author, December 20, 2004.

8. Joseph Clark, former Owen J. Roberts Elementary School principal, conversation with author, February 21, 2008.

9. John Locke, *An Essay Concerning Human Understanding*, http://www. earlymoderntexts.com/assets/pdfs/locke1690book1.pdf (accessed January 4, 2018).

10. Jean Jacques Rousseau, *On the Social Contract*, ed. Roger Masters, trans. Judith Masters (New York: St. Martin's Press, 1978), 46.

11. Jean Jacques Rousseau, *Emile, or On Education*, trans. Allan Bloom (New York: Basic Books, 1979), 37.

12. The anecdote of Schweitzer was one that was presented at an ASCD conference keynote speech delivered by Norman Cousins on March 21, 1977, which the author attended and took notes.

13. John Dewey recognized the dialectic between these two forces in his 1938 book *Experience and Education* (1938; New York: Macmillan Publishing 1963). He wrote, "The history of educational theory is marked by opposition between the idea that education is development from within and that it is formation from without" (p. 17). In 1916 he labeled this dialectic as nurture versus nature when he stated in *Democracy and Education* (1916; New York: Macmillan Publishing, 1966) that "great as is the significance of nurture, of modification, and transformation through direct educational effort, nature, or unlearned capacities, affords the foundation and ultimate resources for such nurture" (p. 117).

14. John Dewey, *The School and the Society, the Child and the Curriculum* (Chicago: University of Chicago Press, 1990), 187.

15. In *Democracy and Education*), John Dewey wrote, "Such a [democratic] society must have a type of education which gives individuals a personal interest in social relationships and control, and habits of mind which secure social changes without introducing disorder" (p. 99).

16. This author made several visits to Meade elementary school in research for *Combating Hatred: Educators Leading the Way* (Lanham MD: Rowman & Littlefield, 2009). This account is based primarily on those visits. However, recent research indicates that this account is also substantially accurate in 2018.

17. Frank Murphy retired in 2010. Many of the innovations that he brought to this school remain as of this writing (2018). See http://thenotebook.org/latest0/2010/06/30/f-goes-public (accessed January 21, 2018) regarding his retirement and http://webgui.phila.k12.pa.us/schools/m/meade (accessed January 21, 2018) for the school's website.

18. Mary Ann Smith, "National Writing Project, It Takes a School," *The Voice* 9, no. 3 (2004), http://www.nwp.org/cs/public/print/resource/1960?x-print_friendly=1 (accessed January 4, 2018).

19. David Warner, "Someplace Special," *Citypaper*, December 19–25, 2002, http://www.citypaper.net/articles/2002-12-19/slant2.shtml (accessed January 18, 2008).

20. The account of Ellen Keyes is a direct firsthand account that occurred while this author was superintendent of the Midview school district (1979–1986).

21. David Jarvie, e-mail message to author, February 8, 2008.

22. Ibid.

23. This author worked for six years with Tom Asad at Normandy High School. These accounts have been verified by Asad.

24. This author worked with Marty Kane for six years at Normandy High School. These accounts have been verified by Kane.

25. Dewey, *The School and the Society, the Child and the Curriculum*, 7.

Chapter Four

Educators Combating Racial Hatred

Black doll hung by noose in high school locker room as "prank."[1]
Coatesville, Pennsylvania, 2017

Incident more hype than reality, Hangman's nooses cause stir in Jena area.[2]
Jena, Louisiana, 2006

HANGING NOOSES IN SCHOOLS:
RACIAL HATRED OR STUDENT PRANKS?

The two quotations that begin this chapter describe two racial incidents involving hanging nooses occurring at high schools 1,250 miles apart. Not only distance but time (eleven years) separates the two. These two incidents dramatically demonstrate that racial hatred can happen anywhere in the country and that time has not bridged the gap between Americans who differ from each other. In both incidents the initial reaction from school officials was that they were not hate crimes but either student pranks or more hype than reality.

Coatesville, the same school district that experienced the exchange of raw racist texts described in the introduction, later witnessed a black baby doll hanging from a ceiling tile in a men's locker room. The superintendent, Cathy Taschner, explained that the doll had been found in the trash by members of the boys cross country team who hid it in the ceiling tile. It was retrieved and found some time later hanging from the locker room ceiling. Learning of this, Tashner interviewed members of the team and determined that it was not a hate crime but rather a "foolish prank."[3] The team was eventually punished by forfeiting their competitions for the remainder of the season.

The story accompanying the Jena, Louisiana, headline began when two nooses were found hanging from a large oak tree that provided the only shade in the school yard. The *Jena Times* called the event an ignorant prank. The school, located in Louisiana's LaSalle parish, had approximately 535 students of whom 85 percent were white. The nooses apparently were hung in response to a black student's question at an assembly as to whether blacks could also sit under the tree—a space traditionally occupied by whites only. The story indicates that the nooses were quietly removed before most students saw them. It also stated that the pranksters were identified and removed from school with a recommendation for expulsion from the principal, Scott Windham. The expulsions were later changed by the expulsion review committee and superintendent, Roy Breithaupt, to three-day suspensions.

This may have been the end of the matter had it not been for a meeting of some black students' parents at a local church to discuss how to respond to the situation. Events of this meeting were reported by another local newspaper, the Alexandria *Town Talk*, which referred to the nooses as a "racial incident."[4] According to the *Jena Times*, this began "a constant barrage of negative media coverage" that prompted school officials to describe the incident as "more media hype than reality."[5]

The incident grew into a crisis, and during the following year a large section of the high school was burned, students were intimidated by a local district attorney, and six black students were charged with attempted murder for the beating of a white student. This last situation was described by the *Washington Post* as "overzealous prosecution of six black high school students charged with beating a white schoolmate."[6] The situation reached a climax when the "'Jena Six' Case Prompt[ed] Mass Demonstrations."[7] It was this prosecution that brought major civil rights leaders, including Jesse Jackson and Al Sharpton, plus thousands of protestors to Jena on September 20, 2007. The crisis was defused in December when the charges against the black students were reduced substantially from attempted murder to second-degree battery.

What is most startling about both the Coatesville and Jena hanging nooses is that the school superintendents did not initially and definitively see the symbolic significance that hanging nooses have on the greater black community. Taschner described the black doll hanging from the ceiling tiles as a "foolish prank." Although later she indicated that "this incident is offensive, insensitive and not reflective of the kind of behavior we expect or will tolerate from our students,"[8] racial incidents continued in the district.

Another episode involving Coatesville students occurred later in the same year when images of pumpkins carved with racist symbols went viral on social media. "Coatesville Students Walk Out in Protest over Racist Pumpkin Carvings" was the October 20, 2017, headline in a section of *The Philadelphia Inquirer*.[9] It once again put the Coatesville school district in the news.

Individuals, presumed to be students of the district, had carved "KKK" and swastikas into pumpkins. Pictures of these flooded social media, which led to a protest by hundreds of school district students.[10] In this case students appeared to be leading the entire community in demanding that racism be dealt with in a substantive and sustained manner.

Superintendent of schools in the LaSalle Parish's Jena High School Roy Briethaupt also did not view the hanging nooses as indicative of a serious racial incident. He was quoted as saying, "In this particular case, I think there is much concern on the part of many people that really has no justification."[11] A child welfare supervisor from the parish who spoke extensively with those students indicated that they did not know about black history and the hanging of black citizens during the South's Jim Crow years following the Civil War. She was quoted as saying, "We discussed this in great detail with those students. They honestly had no knowledge of the history concerning nooses and black citizens."[12] These comments were one of the factors considered when the principal's original recommendation for expulsions was reduced by the superintendent to three days of suspensions. Not everyone agreed.

Some Jena citizens saw the Jena hanging nooses as far more serious. A retired administrator from the LaSalle Parish school district commented, "When the superintendent overruled the principal on expulsion, he sent a message that it wasn't that big of a deal to hang such a hateful symbol of racism and terror in a tree at school."[13] Bill Quigley, writing in *Truthout*, quoted a mother of a Jena High student as saying, "Hanging those nooses was a hate crime, plain and simple."[14] Indeed, hanging nooses are a serious matter and ignorance of the history of their significance can lead to disaster for school leaders as well as entire school districts.

These incidents were reactive to specific events and grew from the lack of an institutionalized sense of social justice. This following case study depicts a situation in the Owen J. Roberts school district that could have become an explosive racial incident. Instead it became an educational opportunity that helped students who played the song "Dixie" at a football game see why it was offensive to black fans.[15]

"DIXIE": TEACHABLE MOMENTS

The civil rights movement of the 1950s, 1960s, and 1970s brought to the surface underlying feelings that Dixie as well as the Confederate flag are often associated with racial segregation and unequal civil rights. It was this association that prompted a black teacher and his friend to protest the Owen J. Roberts High School's playing of "Dixie" at a Friday night football game in the fall of 1998.

They told the principal that they had been personally offended. They were also concerned that many black students may have been offended but were afraid to speak up as they comprised less than 5 percent of the high school population. The principal assured them that the song would not be played again and that he would begin an investigation into the matter.

The principal met with the band director and learned that the song was not officially part of the band's repertoire but that parts of it were spontaneously played by some band members after a hometown touchdown had been scored. The principal told the director to stop this practice. When the director told the students of this decision, some were upset and said that they felt their civil liberties, specifically their First Amendment rights, were being violated. They also told him that they planned to do something about this decision.

This was not an idle threat. The band in this community had a very active booster organization. The self-designated student leader of the group who played "Dixie" was the son of the school board president. These factors eventually landed "Dixie" in the superintendent's lap. I was that superintendent.

The first step taken after discussing the matter with the high school principal and the band director was to contact the teacher who made the protest and assure him that the matter would be investigated and that the song would no longer be played at football games. The next step was to arrange a meeting with the student leader of the band, who will be called Jerry, to discuss the situation.

Jerry came to the meeting well prepared and with a trace of arrogance. He had researched the song and learned that it was a popular one for both the North and the South before and during the Civil War. He pointed out that Abraham Lincoln was fond of it and had it played by military bands at the conclusion of the war.

Jerry could not understand how the song was offensive to anyone and indicated that it had been played at several games with no previous complaints. He stressed that he represented several students who felt their constitutional rights were being violated. After thanking him for his research and interest in the matter, a date was set for another meeting to continue the conversation.

It was troubling to see that this student, a bright young man who obviously possessed leadership potential, was either ignorant of civil rights history or insensitive to the fact that this song could be offensive to some members of the black community. Either conclusion was a condemnation of an educational system that was supposedly preparing future citizens for their participation in a democracy whose strength was built on the recognition of minority as well as majority rights. The situation presented an opportunity for educating not only this young man but also other students and adults who were following this confrontation closely.

It was obvious from the meeting as well as conversations with the principal and band director that Jerry was entrenched in his views. This intransigence was strengthened by the support of his peers. It was clear that a persistent discussion of the black/white racial issue would result in a back-and-forth argument that would not help Jerry or his supporters become more aware of the social justice issues involved.

Because of Jerry's stubbornness on the issue of black/white racism, a less-known topic that contained a similar human rights theme was chosen for future discussions. This was a segment of history regarding the treatment of minority Native Americans by the dominant white culture.

A Book on Native America Racism: *Education for Extinction*

At the next meeting Jerry was given a book to read regarding one aspect of Native American treatment by whites. It was David Wallace Adams's *Education for Extinction*, which is a history of the Native American boarding school experience from 1875 to 1928. This powerful book describes a tragically sad chapter in American history. Many young Native Americans were taken from their families and tribes and relocated to boarding schools hundreds or thousands of miles from their homes.

The main reason for this relocation was that reservation schools, often run by well-intentioned Christian organizations, were not as successful as they might have been. Students would often miss days or weeks at a time, speak in their native languages, and refuse to abandon their cultural traditions.

The boarding school concept solved those problems. It stripped them physically, mentally, and spiritually. They were totally isolated from their families and friends on the reservations.

Their names were changed, often into those of past U.S. presidents or historical figures such as Julius Caesar. They were forbidden to speak their native languages, dress in their customary clothing, discuss their religious beliefs, or mention anything about their cultural traditions. They could speak only English, wore military-style uniforms, listened for hours to sermons about Christianity, and were forced to learn Christian songs and prayers.

Violations of the numerous rules often meant brushing their teeth with strong lye, enduring severe whippings, marching for hours, and suffering other cruel forms of corporal and mental punishment.

Once stripped of their identities, they were reconstructed in the desired image so that they could be assimilated into the white culture. They learned to eat with knives, forks, and spoons. Males were taught farming skills and trades such as carpentry, tinsmithing, and shoemaking. Females spent their time learning proper Victorian skills for women such as sewing, cleaning, ironing, canning, and cooking.

Photos catch the images of transformation. Two particularly potent ones are found on the back of Adams's book. They are provided by the National Anthropological Archives of the Smithsonian Institution and tell the story of a renamed Navajo, Tom Torlino. The photos were taken three years apart. The before picture is of a noble-looking native with long-flowing hair, earrings, a decorative necklace, and traditional Navajo clothing. The after picture is of a groomed young man with short combed hair dressed in a white shirt, tie, and formal jacket.

These contrasting photos show the outward effects of the boarding school program. What they do not capture is the loneliness, heartache, and despair that accompanied many of the transmutations. Adams describes the human tragedies that this program had on both Native American students and their families. He captures the tears, despair, and eventual emptiness endured by many of these natives. At these schools, compassionate treatment was not the goal. Assimilation was.

Hopefully, Adams's dramatic account of these boarding schools would have an impact on Jerry, who was defending "Dixie" as an innocent tune. The next meeting would be a discussion about the book. It would also be about more than that. It would be about "Chief Wahoo."

"Chief Wahoo"

A three-story red-and-white rendition of "Chief Wahoo" stood atop the main entrance of the Cleveland Indians home at Municipal Stadium on the shores of Lake Erie for more than forty years until the Indians moved to a new home in 1994. The sign is currently in the Crawford Auto and Aviation Museum of the Western Reserve Historical Society. While at the stadium, it was set on a large pivot so that it could slowly rotate, showing all angles of the team's chosen mascot.

Angles, indeed. The bright red mascot head, approximately one-third the size of the entire body, is a series of angles—triangular eyes, pointed eyebrows, hooked nose, broad angular grin, sharp chin, slanted ears. All of this is topped off with a peaked feather. Cleveland was one of the founding teams of the American League and began using the mascot name "Indians" in 1915. The Wahoo logo was adopted shortly after World War II and remains in prominent use to this day even though it will no longer be on the Indians' uniforms beginning in 2019. Many Clevelanders were embarrassed, especially during a pennant or World Series chase, when widespread media attention sent Wahoo grinning around the world. Nonetheless, passion for the chief has been strong over the years.

An event in 1998 revealed the depth of that passion. It occurred at an annual conference of United Methodists that was held in Cleveland at which a resolution was introduced urging the members of the church to stop wearing clothing or hats displaying the logo. One woman was quoted by Cleveland's daily newspaper, the *Plain Dealer*, as saying, "I would cease being a United Methodist before I would cease wearing my Chief Wahoo clothing."[16] With this in mind, let us return for a second meeting between Jerry and the school superintendent.

At the second meeting Jerry was given a baseball cap featuring the grinning "Wahoo." When asked how he felt about the logo, he admitted that it looked rather silly. He was also given a copy of an editorial cartoon by the famous *Philadelphia Inquirer* editorial cartoonist Tony Auth.

The cartoon is from October 22, 1997, and is titled "Can You Imagine?" It contains a drawing of "Chief Wahoo" with the words "The Cleveland INDIANS." Next to this is a rendition of a smiling Asian labeled "The Cleveland ASIANS." Two other drawings and labels complete the cartoon: a grinning African with the words "The Cleveland AFRICANS" and a beaming Hispanic in a sombrero labeled "The Cleveland HISPANICS."

This cartoon had a noticeable impact on Jerry, who agreed that the Asian, African, and Hispanic logos would be offensive and should not be used by a major league team. He was still a little undecided about the Indians but was beginning to see that it may also be offensive. Jerry did admit that the Native American boarding schools were an ugly chapter in American history.

When asked if he would wear the baseball cap, Jerry said that to wear it in the presence of Native Americans would probably be offensive to them. To wear it in front of others could be offensive only if they were politically correct individuals. To wear it alone in the woods would not offend anyone. But what would this say about his true feelings? No easy answer.

Jerry saw the social justice principle contained in the "Chief Wahoo" example. He began to apply it to the playing of "Dixie." He agreed that it was possible for those who may have experienced racial discrimination and whose ancestors may have suffered from more than 350 years of slavery and the Jim Crow Black Codes to be offended by the song. The meeting ended, and for all practical purpose the matter was closed.

One more step was necessary: to share some aspects of this learning experience with teachers, students, and the greater community. For this purpose I prepared an article titled "'Chief Wahoo,' or 'Should I Wear My Hat,' or 'Dixie Revisited' (You Choose)."[17] It began by telling of fond childhood memories of "Chief Wahoo." It continued by describing some of the impact that Adams's book had on ways of viewing Native Americans. Auth's cartoon was depicted, and the question as to whether or not a person should wear the "Chief Wahoo" cap was asked. The article concluded with connections to the "Dixie" episode. It was distributed to teachers and board members and published on the school district's website.

The "Dixie" case study presents one example of ways of combating racial hatred by viewing it as a teaching/learning opportunity. The band's playing

"Dixie" and the complaint of a minority faculty member presented special teachable moments. These were an opening to educate students, teachers, and the general public. This is an example of reacting to a crisis that ended with positive results. There are times, such as this example, when it is necessary to be reactive. In situations concerning social justice issues, it is far better to be proactive rather than reactive.

To be proactive places a special responsibility on school leaders and teachers. It demands the development of a curriculum and a school environment that is rich in its consideration of multicultural perspectives. Only through carefully planned educational programs can progress be made in combating the ignorance that often surrounds human rights issues. These programs should involve recognizing racial isolation and building bridges across racial divides that exist both between and within many communities.

The following two case studies are examples of building such bridges. The first describes ways some teachers and students in one of Cleveland's overwhelmingly white suburbs encountered an amazing mission settlement in one of Cleveland's worst ghettos, an area that was nearly destroyed by violent racial riots in 1966. The second relates ways that members of a community came together to help tear down racial barriers in the Owen J. Roberts school district.

BUILDING BRIDGES ACROSS RACIAL DIVIDES

Sister Henrietta and Our Lady of Fatima Parish Mission

The most serious riots in Cleveland's history began on July 18, 1966. They started in an urban region known as Hough, a two-square-mile area that went from a predominantly white middle-class neighborhood in 1950 to a predominantly nonwhite one in 1960.[18] Before the Ohio National Guard was able to restore calm seven days after the riots began, four people had been killed, thirty seriously injured, and nearly three hundred arrested. More than 240 fires had turned the area into something that resembled a war zone.

Many people, fearful of their lives, fled Hough following the first gunshots and fires. A sixty-four-year-old nun refused to leave the mission where she worked at East 68th Street and Quimby Avenue. Her name was Sister Henrietta. She was an inspiration to many people in the Hough area because of her charitable work—work that improved the lives of hundreds of distressed children, women, and men. These people were the ones who formed a protective circle around her. It must have been a truly remarkable sight to see this relatively short woman stand tall in her full white habit against the violence that was engulfing the neighborhood.

Sister Henrietta's career was in nursing. She graduated from Canton's Mercy Hospital School of Nursing in 1925. That same year she entered the religious order of the Sisters of Charity of Saint Augustine and took her final vows in 1931. She became a supervisor of nurses and an administrator at Mercy Hospital until she left to become director of nursing services at Cleveland's Saint Vincent Charity Hospital in 1962. In 1965 she left the hospital and moved to a humble Hough area parish known as Our Lady of Fatima.

In the mid-1960s Our Lady of Fatima was more than a local parish serving Catholic families. A large number of Catholics had moved from the area, and Our Lady of Fatima became a social mission to serve the people of Cleveland's worst urban ghetto.

The parish's pastor, Father Albert Koklowsky, was known for his outspoken writings that appeared in the Cleveland diocese's *Catholic Universe Bulletin*. An example of his passionate voice is found in a quotation from his column titled "A Voice from the Slums" in which he wrote:

> What I have to write is not pleasant, because I live in a ghetto.
> Here my people and I move in a nightmare in a festering junkyard.
> Ghettos are created by men for the less fortunate, the least lovable.
> My ghetto is a creation of the Great Society which has forgotten how to love and how to pity. Here the almighty dollar takes precedence over human dignity.
> In the ghetto where I live, the littered, glass-strewn streets separate the trampled, grassless lawns. Dirty papers rustle on the pavement and tumble into corners.
> Sidewalks are spotted with stinking mattresses, rusty springs, crumbling furniture. Garbage and rubbish pickups are slow, slow, slow.
> There are odors—57 varieties—stomach-flipping stenches. Our backyards are jammed with junk and cans and paper and rats. [19]

Words such as these resonated with Sister Henrietta. Her reason for leaving hospital life was simple. She came to a realization that her antiseptically clean life within a manmade bubble was not the encounter with the world that she read in Christ's gospel message. So she left and joined Father Koklowsky's mission. [20]

One of the major programs that Sister Henrietta started soon after arriving at Our Lady of Fatima was known as Caridad, Spanish for charity and an acronym for Charity and Responsibility in Deed and Duty. Caridad, consisting primarily of Hough-area women, organized programs dealing with health care, cleanliness, and disease prevention. It also established food, clothing, and furniture banks for neighborhood residents. Caridad's constitution echoed and expanded the words of our Declaration of Independence in stating that "our neighbors have the right to life in the mainstream of America, to liberty from debilitating disease and poverty, to the pursuit of happiness with decent education and employment." [21]

Perhaps the most dramatic project that Sister Henrietta started was known as Famicos. This program, still in existence, was her response to urban high-rise housing developments that she labeled "vertical filing cabinets for people."[22]

Famicos was a very energetic program that involved the men of the neighborhood and revealed a Sister Henrietta who was as tough as nails. Slogans symbolizing Famicos's goals were to "make every house a home" and "improve, don't move."[23]

Some of Famicos's projects included providing financial advice and doing house maintenance/improvement work. More important was its home leasing and ownership program. This involved organizing neighborhood men to rebuild houses after Sister Henrietta worked to get them condemned by the city.

After the houses were thoroughly renovated, they were leased to families for low monthly rents that were used to help pay the renovation debts. After the debts were repaid in approximately fifteen years, the family had the option of taking ownership for a nominal cost. As of 1995 approximately 450 houses had been renovated and leased this way.[24] Sister Henrietta was helped greatly in these efforts by the volunteer work of Robert Wolf, a vice president for B. F. Goodrich, who gave up his job to work with the Famicos project.

The effects of this program were amazing to see. Several blocks of well-maintained houses with neat landscaping stood out as an oasis in the midst of 1970s urban blight. The idea of organizing neighborhoods so that residents could be empowered was somewhat unique at this time.

Sister Henrietta's impact in both community organizing and improving racial relations was recognized by awards that include the Catholic Interracial Council Award, the National Urban Coalition's Distinguished Community Service Award, and the American Jewish Committee's Micah Award. Another great impact of hers, one not recognized by awards or well known beyond a few individuals, was the inspiration that she gave to a small group of teachers and students from the all-white Normandy High School that was located in the suburb of Parma, Ohio.

Experience in Free Form Education

Normandy High School opened in the fall of 1968. It was the newest and most innovative of Parma's three high schools. The principal, Wesley Gaab, and the assistant principal, Marty Kane, were constantly seeking better ways to make learning come alive for the more than 2,700 students attending the school in the early 1970s. One of the programs that they initiated was called Experience in Free Form Education (EFFE).

Wes Gaab introduced the EFFE idea to approximately 135 Normandy teachers at a faculty meeting in the fall of 1971. It was an ambitious idea that entailed abolishing the entire high school curriculum for one week and replacing it with hands-on courses conducted both at the school and in the greater community. Teachers could develop courses that they had always wanted to teach but could not because of bureaucratic restraints. Once courses were developed and approved, Gaab and Kane developed an entirely new master schedule and opened registration for students.

Some courses were held in the school and consisted of an extensive array of community and business speakers. Many involved extended trips that incorporated weekends and lasted up to nine days. Examples of these included an in-depth study of theater in New York City and environmental studies of the Mississippi delta in Louisiana. Others utilized regional community resources such as a course on criminal studies that involved lectures from attorneys and visitations to courtrooms and prisons.

Four social studies teachers at Normandy High School developed a course on the city of Cleveland that was designed to provide sociological experiences that students could not get from lectures or textbooks while sitting in their all-white suburban classrooms. These teachers along with twenty-five students explored the city for five days in unbelievably rich ways.

One of these involved listening to VISTA volunteers in a Hispanic outreach center in Cleveland's West Side describe why it costs more to be poor. Another was learning about the Bureau of Indian Affairs' policy of assimilation by visiting the Cleveland American Indian Education Center on Denison Avenue. Cleveland's Chinese neighborhood on Rockwell and the Little Italy area centered in Murray Hill near Case Western Reserve University were other sites visited.

One of the speakers in Little Italy shocked most of the group when he described how it was possible to fill the area with armed men from the suburbs in case any African Americans tried moving into the neighborhood. This comment set a dramatic backdrop for the most memorable encounter, an in-depth visit with Sister Henrietta in Hough.

None of the students had ever been to an urban ghetto. Few had any previous substantive contact with African Americans. They listened in astonishment as Sister Henrietta opened an unknown world for them.

She described the horror of finding a woman who had been dead for several days being eaten by rats. She described children going to school with different shoes on their left and right feet, children not ashamed but grateful that they had shoes at all. She told of high rents being charged by slum landlords for apartments in houses that had been subdivided many times. She explained that these same houses had inadequate plumbing and antiquated heating systems. This meant that many residents were very cold, while others within the same house had to open windows to keep from roasting.

After sharing these and other stories Sister Henreitta described her work in founding both Caridad and Famicos. Students accompanied her on walks through the neighborhood and saw the "Spic 'n' Span" award signs for meeting cleanliness standards proudly displayed in many windows. They visited food and clothing banks, talked with volunteers, and were impressed as they walked by some of Famicos's renovated houses nestled in the urban wasteland.

Most students were somber if not totally silent on their forty-five-minute trip back to their safe suburban school. When they did speak, the words came from a confused mix of disbelief and empathy. Eyes had been opened. Bridges had been built. As the months and years unfolded, many of these young adults referred back to the EFFE week as one of the most powerful of their lives.

The vision of the short, relatively old, supposedly frail Sister Henrietta—a woman who challenged social injustices in a small part of the world—was an inspiration to teachers and students in Ohio. She helped build bridges across a racial divide. Teachers, administrators, and board members in the Owen J. Roberts school district in Southeastern Pennsylvania also built bridges to help tear down the racial isolation in their community.

Camp Confidence

Both insensitivity to racial issues and racial isolation were realities in the Owen J. Roberts school district in the early 1990s. Newstell Marable, head of the local chapter of the National Association for the Advancement of Colored People, had worked for years to get the district to recognize Martin Luther King Jr. Day. It was finally recognized as a holiday for students but not employees in the late 1980s. Teachers preferred using this day for in-service so that they could begin summer break one day earlier. It was not until several years later that they reluctantly agreed to honor this day.

Marable was also concerned that many residents in the Park Springs Federal Housing Development felt isolated from the rest of the district. Approximately 5 percent of the district's 3,800 students were classified as African American in 1990. Most of these were concentrated in Park Springs, which was located on the outskirts of the district. It was apparent from several comments that many district residents would gladly permit this area to be annexed by the neighboring district—if it wanted them.

To begin changing this attitude meant establishing links with as many Park Springs students and residents as was possible. As the new superintendent in the district, I decided to ride the school bus with students on the first day of school. This move began establishing contacts with several residents that, over the next few weeks, grew into conversations.

One conversation that was particularly important occurred with the director of Park Springs, Kevin Lanning. It happened at a football game when he asked if it might be possible to extend the free and reduced school lunch program into the summer. More than 95 percent of Park Springs students were on the federal free and reduced lunch and breakfast programs. Lanning pointed out something that should have been obvious to everyone: these students needed free nutritious meals year 'round and not just for the nine months that school was in session. He then explained that summertime was a real problem for students and other residents of Park Springs.

Federal housing development residents were not permitted to have pets. They could not plant gardens. Playgrounds were essentially barren. As for swimming, the nearest pool was several miles away in Spring City. Youths generally did not have transportation to Spring City or the daily two-dollar entrance fee. These were serious concerns for Lanning, who wondered about the effects of placing students into the pressure cooker of Philadelphia-area high temperatures and humidity with inadequate nourishment and little or no physical or mental relief.

These concerns formed the nucleus for a summer camp for students who could not afford to experience a traditional one. The schools had cafeterias, playgrounds, libraries, land for gardens, and a swimming pool, all of which were idle during the summer. Over the next few months, several district administrators, school board members, and community residents designed a summer camp for Park Springs and other students who lacked resources to attend a traditional summer camp. It began in the summer of 1992 and was called Camp Confidence.

Camp Confidence was a free camp for students who had little, if any, money for a traditional camp experience. In order to minimize community criticism regarding the expenditure of public monies, no local tax dollars were used to run the camp. Instead it relied on personal donations of time and money as well as some special state funds that were secured through a grant.

The camp, designed for approximately one hundred elementary and middle school aged youngsters, lasted for approximately six weeks and was held in the district's middle school. It ran from approximately 9:30 in the morning until 2:00 in the afternoon and included a free lunch for the students. The middle school was chosen as the site because it contained a swimming pool and had many unused acres surrounding it. The school's assistant principal agreed to oversee the camp, and certified teachers both within and outside of the district donated their services.

Classroom activities during camp stressed nontraditional approaches to reading and language arts such as puppet theaters, plays, and computer activities. District librarians established a special collection of high-interest books. Physical education teachers designed noncompetitive games for students of different age levels. Field trips were considered of key importance, and several focused on environmental and cultural topics. Leadership skills were developed for many participants who in subsequent years became peer counselors for younger campers in the program.

The camp received wide support from school personnel, citizens, and those doing business with the district. One important contribution was from the district's contracted transportation provider, who donated daily buses to transport students from Park Springs to the middle school as well as for several field trips during the six-week experience. Other donations included the services of local farmers, organized by a school board member. They plowed plots of land near the middle school so that students could plant individual gardens. Swimming was provided for each student at least two days per week.

While students were attending the camp, their parents were not forgotten. Strengthening home-school relationships was a core principle of the camp philosophy. One of the conditions for students being able to attend the camp was that their parents agreed to attend various sessions held at Park Springs.

These meetings were coordinated by the director of Park Springs and included open discussions led by trained school guidance counselors. They focused on various problems and included discussions on home-school communications, student susceptibility to illegal drugs, problems associated with gang cultures, and other parenting concerns.

The sessions increased parent support for the camp and built a sense of community among participants. This was evident on the "graduation day," when parents and community members attended a special program that recognized each student's special contribution to the camp. A brief ceremony was followed by a spaghetti lunch for students, parents, teachers, administrators, school board members, and invited citizens. The lunch was prepared by students with the help of teachers and featured some of the produce that was grown in the campers' gardens.

Camp Confidence was different from most summer school programs that have grown in recent years as a result of various federal and state programs. There were no pre- or post-tests, no scripted programs used by remediation teachers, and no fears of failure. Camp Confidence students developed reading and math skills while having fun-filled active camp experiences designed to bolster their positive self-esteem. They genuinely liked the camp.

One eight-year-old stated in an article in the *Philadelphia Inquirer* that if he was not "attending Camp Confidence, he would be home sleeping or watching TV."[25] These positive sentiments were echoed by a nine-year-old who said, "It gives you something to do. I like using the computers. They're fun."[26] Teachers and others associated with the program also felt it was very worthwhile. Camp teachers shared many accounts of the camp with their colleagues during district-wide opening teachers' meetings. One of the farmers who plowed land at the middle school for student gardens was also a school board member. He gave several positive reports on the camp experience at public school board meetings.

Camp Confidence was a bridge across a racial divide that brought Park Springs students and families more completely into the school district community. The relationships that developed between district personnel, the director, and residents of Park Springs carried over into the regular school year. The camp spurred additional outreach efforts that resulted in elementary after-school programs, ongoing parent meetings, and the installation of a computer lab at Park Springs.

Perhaps the greatest benefit from the Camp Confidence experience was that it opened many people's eyes and created different perspectives regarding the needs of disadvantaged students who were clustered in an isolated section of the district—students who also happened to be mostly African American.

Opening eyes and creating new perspectives—this is a common theme that runs through this segment of the chapter:

- Encountering the racial effects of "Dixie": revealing self-righteousness and helping others see the hurtfulness that can be inflicted through the playing of a supposedly innocent song at a football game;
- EFFE: working to bridge a racial divide created by de facto segregation by bringing students from an all-white suburban high school into contact with a mission that served people living in an urban ghetto; and
- Camp Confidence: seeing the reality of racial isolation within a community and creating a bond that brought diverse people together.

These perspectives are created by proactive actions, in sharp contrast to the hanging nooses described at the chapter's opening.

Two important educational theories can be associated with opening eyes and developing new perspectives. One is deconstruction, and the other is critical pedagogy.

PRACTICE AND THEORY: DECONSTRUCTION AND CRITICAL PEDAGOGY

Working Definitions for Educational Practitioners

To effectively combat racial hatred, school practitioners need to become critical pedagogues who understand and use the process of deconstruction. Deconstruction's roots are found in the famous French philosopher Jacques Derrida's numerous books and lectures. Deconstruction concepts are manifested in other disciplines as well. For example, they are found in Terry Eagleton's literary criticism and Rem Koolhaas's architecture. "Deconstruction" is a term that is currently popular among many educational theorists, where it is often associated with critical pedagogy. Some prominent critical pedagogues include Paulo Freire, Jeanne Brady, Michael Apple, Ira Shor, Peter McLaren, and Henry Giroux.

Even though numerous books have been written on deconstruction, it is difficult to find a precise definition of the term. Derrida himself resisted defining or labeling it. Instead he demonstrated through his writing and lectures a process of carefully examining items, such as Paul Celan's poem "Aschenglorie." In scrutinizing this poem, Derrida would deconstruct each word's components and etymology. At the conclusion it was as if the poem was lying in numerous little bits on a table. The meaning was there to be reconstructed by individuals in their own unique ways. This is a liberating process that can yield complex meanings and varied interpretations free from rigid interpretations imposed by others.

It is easier to find definitions of critical pedagogy for educational practitioners in a democratic society. Ira Shor offers one in terms of empowerment. He stated that "empowering education . . . is a critical-democratic pedagogy for self and social change."[27] He wrote further that "the goals of this pedagogy are to relate personal growth to public life, by developing strong skills, academic knowledge, habits of inquiry and critical curiosity about society, power, inequality and change."[28]

These goals can be achieved by becoming critically conscious of how we view ourselves in rethinking both knowledge and our societal relationships.[29] Shor identified four qualities of critical consciousness as power awareness, critical literacy, permanent desocialization, and self-education/organization. His definition of permanent desocialization is particularly helpful in providing a working definition of critical pedagogy for educational practitioners. He defined it as:

> understanding and challenging artificial, political limits on human development; questioning power and inequality in the status quo; examining socialized values in consciousness and in society which hold back democratic change in individuals and in the larger culture; seeing self and social transformation as a joint process . . . [and] nurturing a passion for justice and a concern for the environment, for the community and for public life.[30]

The purpose of this chapter is not to elaborate further on theoretical definitions of either deconstruction or critical pedagogy but rather to develop practical understandings of both as processes of discovery and illumination that can help practitioners become effective leaders in encountering social justice issues. This will be done through two illustrations. The first will be a generalized activity that defines deconstruction, and the second will be a practical illustration of ways that a critical pedagogue might use the deconstruction process from a social justice perspective.

Deconstructing Musical Lyrics

Musical lyrics can provide rich and interesting material for helping to define the concept of deconstruction. Imagine leading a professional development session in which you wanted to build a community of learners while at the same time teaching the concept of deconstruction. As a school leader you decided that both of these elements are important for later professional development sessions when you will examine several books and other experiences.

One example using musical lyrics can be using a song familiar to most Americans (and many foreigners): Simon and Garfunkel's "Sound of Silence." While the tune has become part of our American culture, the words are less familiar. Let us assume that you have a group of approximately twenty-five teachers (any level), school leaders, students, or others who are sitting in a circle. Play the song for them without a copy of the words. Then play it again giving them copies of the words. They will notice a big difference and discover words that they had not previously understood or even knew were there.

Now play it a third time and have them circle one line of the poetry that is most significant for them. Finally play it a fourth time and have them circle one word that has the most meaning to them. The group is now ready to share their lines and/or words and the reasons that they chose them. Their choices will be remarkable to you and members of the group as to the similarities and differences. It will also be eye opening as individuals learn much about members of the group that they had not known previously. You could then explain that this activity demonstrates the concept of deconstruction and that you could take it further if you wanted to go into different words to explore their etymology and cultural significance. Another deconstruction illustration that involves social justice issues can be found in the Philadelphia Phillies's giveaway at the last regular season game of 2007.

Phillies MVP Giveaway

The final home game of the regular season for the professional major league baseball team the Philadelphia Phillies is known as Fan Appreciation Day. In 2007 the giveaway for fans attending the game was a large poster of the National League's Most Valuable Player, Jimmy Rollins. When seen from a distance, the thirteen-by-eighteen-inch poster shows Jimmy, an African American, in a running pose. He is wearing sunglasses, batting gloves, and his red and white home uniform, which prominently displays number 11 on his left shoulder.

When examined closely, the picture changes dramatically. Rather than one photo of Jimmy, there are 1,485 smaller images of team members in various poses taken in their home stadium, Citizens Bank Park. What appeared to be one thing from a distance turned out to be something far more complex when examined in greater detail. Rather than one player we see a composite of the team. Seeing the smaller images in relationship to the whole is the beginning of deconstructing the poster.

A critical pedagogue would deconstruct the poster further and dig deeply into its context. What might such a pedagogue see? Jimmy Rollins's African American heritage almost begs for an examination of the history of race relations relative to professional baseball. This study would reveal the effects that the National Association of Base Ball Players, the first organized professional league, had when it denied the Philadelphia Pythians, an all-black team, admittance to the league in 1867 because of the team's race. This professional major league color barrier was not broken until Jackie Robinson played for the Brooklyn Dodgers in 1947.

The key role played by Latinos in helping to break this color barrier would probably be another area for consideration and study. Today players of different races, nationalities, and ethnicities are chosen to play together based on their talent and not the color of their skin or the slant of their eyes. The same cannot be said regarding gender.

The critical pedagogue would probably notice that there are no females among the 1,485 photos in the Phillies giveaway poster. This question of gender equity may lead to a study of the history of females and professional baseball that would tell the story of the All-American Girls Baseball League, a name later changed to the American Girls Baseball League.

This league was started during World War II when nearly one-half of the professional male players were in military service. The league was fairly popular with teams such as the Racine Belles, the Milwaukee Chicks, and the South Bend Blue Sox drawing almost one million fans in 1948. This popularity waned with the end of the war, and the league folded in 1953. Its story was popularized in the 1992 movie *A League of Their Own* starring Tom Hanks, Rosie O'Donnell, Geena Davis, and Madonna. There was some interest in having some of the female stars join men's professional baseball until major league commissioner Ford Frick barred them in 1952—a ban that lasts until this day.

Deconstructing further, the critical pedagogue might notice that two of the 1,485 images are of Philadelphia's relatively new stadium. Inquiries about this would reveal that the site was selected after a bitter battle in which then mayor John Street tried to have the stadium located in the central part of the city, which would have taken land that formed the heart of Philadelphia's

Chinatown. After an outcry from the to-be-displaced population and its sympathizers, the location was moved to the Sports Complex in South Philadelphia.

A study of the stadium would also reveal that the right to name the 43,647-seat ballpark was part of a twenty-five-year contract given to Citizens Bank in exchange for $95,000,000. This fact might prompt questions regarding the ways that huge financial empires have grown from broadcast rights, merchandising, advertising, and other financial arrangements that have turned America's pastime into a multibillion dollar business.

The power of money definitely affects the game. For instance, vast sums are used to buy and sell players who are often treated as commodities on the open market. They, in turn, fiercely compete for the golden ring of superstar status. This competition leads some of them to take performance-enhancing drugs that, in certain cases, have resulted in public hearings before the U.S. Congress and negative publicity for the entire sport. At this point other questions may arise for the critical pedagogue. These might concern the role of Congress in these investigations and the intersection of private enterprise with public policy.

Another point of interest regarding the stadium that may be raised by the critical pedagogue's deconstruction is the fact that it cost $346,000,000 with 51 percent coming from public funds and 49 from private investment. This division of funding would probably raise questions regarding public expenditures and the ways they often serve special interests and not the general population. With single ticket prices ranging from $150 (the Diamond Club) to $20 (standing room only), prepaid parking costing $18 and relatively expensive food ($3.75 hot dogs and $7.75 beers), there is little chance that economically distressed Philadelphians can afford to attend many games. Perhaps this explains the fact that fans at most games are predominantly white.

These are only some examples of ways a critical pedagogue concerned with the manifestation of social justice ideals in a democracy might deconstruct this simple yet incredibly complex poster. Deconstruction is a challenging process. It demands an interdisciplinary approach and a strong knowledge base.

In deconstructing the poster, the critical pedagogue journeyed through the disciplines of history, political science, sociology, and economics. The synthesis of these disciplines adds new dimensions and contributes to a fuller awareness of the poster's representations. This awareness has the potential of helping the pedagogue construct fresh meanings that may not have been possible prior to the deconstruction. These new perspectives aid in making judgments that may guide future actions, especially as regards social justice issues.

An interdisciplinary journey through deconstruction is oftentimes blocked by paradigms that exist in each discipline. There is the danger that these paradigms might exclude perceptions that could lead to different perspectives and enlightened actions.[31] A strong interdisciplinary knowledge base is essential to overcome these barriers.

For educational practitioners who hope to act as critical pedagogues, the knowledge base must go beyond the material that is usually found in traditional educational courses such as educational theory, strategic planning, assessment, curriculum development, instructional supervision, finance, policy development, and public relations. It must also include a broad knowledge of the liberal arts including studies of literature, foreign cultures and languages, history, political science, economics, sociology, philosophy, religion, and the arts. Such knowledge is not static and needs to be continuously refreshed through awareness of international, national, and current events.

Even though a broad liberal arts knowledge base will help the practitioner/critical pedagogue analyze social justice issues in a democratic society, it does not necessarily provide two essential qualities associated with critical analysis and skillful deconstruction. These particular qualities are an open-mindedness that permits interdisciplinary investigation and a knowledge and understanding of democratic ideals that serve as a lighthouse to guide it. This lighthouse can also lead the practitioner/critical pedagogue in synthesizing the results of the deconstruction so that educational strategies can be created to further social justice ideals.

ESSENTIAL QUALITIES: OPEN-MINDEDNESS AND KNOWLEDGE OF DEMOCRATIC VALUES

Open-Mindedness

Open-mindedness is an essential quality for the practitioner/critical pedagogue. This is not easy to achieve as our minds continuously create constructs. This is a necessary phenomenon as these constructs enable us to function in a multisensory world. Some of these constructs are permeable, but many are nearly impermeable. George Kelly, in his book *A Theory of Personality: The Psychology of Personal Constructs*, differentiates between permeable and impermeable constructs. He wrote:

> A construct is permeable if it will admit to its range of convenience new elements which are not yet construed within its framework. An utterly concrete construct, if there were such a thing, would not be permeable at all, for it would be made up of certain specified elements—those and no others. Such a construct would have to be impermeable.[32]

It is important for effective practitioner/critical pedagogues to understand this differentiation.

Both permeable and impermeable constructs are necessary for individuals to function effectively. Permeable constructs enable us to deal with changing situations while impermeable ones are the anchors that secure our beliefs and values. Effective practitioner/critical pedagogues recognize the value and limitations of each and strike a balance between the two.

In addition to anchoring beliefs and values, impermeable constructs can bind and enslave individuals as they prevent open-mindedness. An example of the latter taken from literature provides an illustration that can be helpful in leading to this understanding. It involves the character Benjy from William Faulkner's novel *The Sound and the Fury*.

Faulkner's *The Sound and the Fury* is a novel set in fictional Yoknapatawpha County during the 1920s. It is a complex story that deals with timelessness and resistance to change in a part of the Antebellum South still dominated by the power of formerly aristocratic plantation families. The Compsons, ragged but nonetheless intact, try to hold onto a past that valued above all the power that came to them as landed gentry from the economic and social rigidity of the slave system. Faulkner brilliantly captures the concepts of impermeable constructs and resistance to change in his description of a member of the Compson family, Benjy.

Benjy is an imbecilic character—a large thirty-three-year-old man with a three-year-old mind. His body continues to grow and change; his mind does not. Benjy's strongest construct, an impermeable one, is of his sister Caddy. She is the member of the family who cares deeply about Benjy, and he cares deeply for her. Especially pleasurable for him are the times that they spent together outdoors. Because of these memories, Benjy perceived in his most primordial sense, his sense of smell, that "Caddy smelled like trees."[33]

Benjy, confused about time, is unaware of the fact that Caddy has been gradually maturing. It is only when there is an outward manifestation of that change, Caddy wearing perfume for the first time, that Benjy reacts. Unable to accept change in one of his most impermeable constructs, he bellows and cries like a baby. This is very disturbing to the entire family but especially to his mother, Miss Caroline, who is lying upstairs in a near-perpetual state of sickness with a cloth on her head. No one can quiet Benjy until Caddy realizes the source of the problem and washes off the perfume. Benjy stops bawling because, as Faulkner describes it, Caddy once again "smelled like trees."[34]

There are many lessons regarding open-mindedness as well as permeable and impermeable constructs in this illustration. Benjy's impermeable construct of Caddy works two ways. Caddy is the one he loves. She cares for him and gives him pleasurable moments. This love grounds his world of experiences and makes him happy.

At the same time, this impermeable construct binds him to the Caddy that was created in his infantile three-year-old mind. He is, in effect, blinded with regard to Caddy. Lacking permeability in this construct prevents him from being open-minded and recognizing changes that are taking place in her. When he smells these changes, he rebels in the most powerful way that he knows—by bellowing like a baby. Being blinded by an impermeable construct and reacting in an irrational, often emotional, outburst can be referred to as a Benjy reaction.

This illustration has many lessons for practitioner/critical pedagogues who desire to deal with social justice issues. Effectiveness in dealing with such issues demands that, first of all, practitioners recognize that they themselves have impermeable Benjy constructs that both ground their values and can also prevent them from being open-minded. These constructs should be continuously examined and assessed relative to both the highest social justice ideals and their concept of open-mindedness. This self-reflection is often difficult and requires that individuals periodically need to view themselves from a stranger's perspective. Continuous self-reflection may help them avoid Benjy reactions.

Second, practitioner/critical pedagogues need to be aware that other individuals have impermeable Benjy constructs that also both ground their values and prohibit their open-mindedness in certain circumstances. These need to be understood and strategies need to be developed to deal with them so as to create greater flexibility if their impermeable constructs are blocking attainment of social justice ideals. This is especially important when confronting hatred based on racial prejudice as hatred is usually irrational and deep seated. Creating this flexibility is a critical factor in minimizing Benjy reactions.

Third, it is important to realize that institutions are usually collective extensions of individuals' beliefs and values. These institutions dictate the ways in which we educate our children, make laws and judge our citizens, conduct economic activities, care for our sick and infirm, and generally interact as citizens of a democratic society. These institutions also contain impermeable Benjy constructs that usually have developed over many years, oftentimes growing from painful conflicts and compromises.

As with individuals, an institution's Benjy constructs need to be understood and strategies developed so that institutions are continuously renewed to manifest a democratic society's highest social justice ideals. Such renewal should also aim to avoid as many Benjy reactions as possible. Achieving democracy's highest social justice ideals becomes the goal.

Social justice ideals are the critical criteria that measure personal, individual, and institutional values. A powerful metaphor for these ideals is the beacon light found atop a lighthouse. As a beacon guides sailors past hidden dangers safely into the harbor, social justice ideals should guide a practitioner/critical pedagogue's deconstruction of situations and events concerning social justice issues.

The same ideals should also direct the practitioner in synthesizing the results of the deconstruction so that strategies can be developed and actions taken to further their attainment. For enlightened educators in a democracy, the ideals comprising this beacon come from the documented beliefs that form the foundation of the democracy itself. As such they need to be examined, understood, and cultivated on a continuous basis.

Knowledge of Democratic Ideals

In a democratic society a practitioner/critical pedagogue's impermeable values should flow from the stated ideals of the democracy itself. Consideration of such ideals through meditation is presented in chapter 1. Reviewing these should include deliberation of at least four important sources of democratic ideals: the Declaration of Independence, the Constitution of the United States, the "Four Freedoms" that were identified by Franklin Roosevelt during World War II, and the United Nations Declaration of Human Rights.

Drawing heavily on the philosophy of John Locke and his beliefs that the source of government in a democratic society flows from each individual person, the Declaration of Independence states in a most concise way some of the basic ideals of our democratic society. Nowhere are these ideals summarized as succinctly as in the beginning of the second paragraph of the Declaration, which reads, "We hold these truths to be self-evident, that all men are created equal, that they are endowed by their Creator with certain unalienable rights, that among these are Life, Liberty and the pursuit of Happiness."[35]

These basic rights are expanded in the Constitution of the United States by the first ten amendments also known as the Bill of Rights. These amendments guarantee, among others, the freedoms of speech, press, religion, and assembly. They also protect individuals from unreasonable searches and seizures and assure those accused of crimes the right to a fair and speedy trial.[36] The Constitution provides for the continuous evolution of basic rights through the amendment process. The purpose of this built-in evolutionary process is to fulfill the purpose of forming "a more perfect union."[37]

An example of this evolutionary process is clearly seen in the Thirteenth, Fourteenth, and Fifteenth Amendments following the Civil War that are known as the Reconstruction Amendments. These concern the abolition of slavery, the establishment of due process, and the granting of voting rights for former slaves. Many of these guarantees were circumvented by Jim Crow laws in the former Confederacy that were not addressed until the Civil Rights Act of 1964 and the Voting Rights Act of 1965.

Ideals important in our democracy have come from sources other than the Declaration and the Constitution. One important source is the "Four Freedoms" speech that Franklin Roosevelt gave to the U.S. Congress on January 6, 1941. This speech summarized some of the goals for which we were fighting World War II and pictured a future world that guaranteed freedom of speech and expression, freedom of every person to worship God in his or her own way, freedom from want, and freedom from fear.[38]

The social justice ideals expressed in these "Four Freedoms" found further manifestation in the Universal Declaration of Human Rights endorsed by the United States and adopted by the General Assembly of the United Nations on December 10, 1948. The Preamble for this document begins by recognizing that "inherent dignity and . . . equal and inalienable rights of all members of the human family [are] the foundation of freedom, justice and peace in the world."[39]

Following the Universal Declaration's Preamble, there are thirty articles outlining basic ideals that are the birthright of all of the world's peoples. Important for consideration in this chapter is Article 1 that reads, "All human beings are born free and equal in dignity and rights. They are endowed with reason and conscience and should act towards one another in a spirit of brotherhood."[40] Article 26 is also important. It states, "Education shall be directed to the full development of the human personality and to the strengthening of respect for human rights and fundamental freedoms. It shall promote understanding, tolerance and friendship among all nations, racial or religious groups, and shall further the activities of the United Nations for the maintenance of peace."[41]

Taken together these four documents—the Declaration of Independence, the Constitution of the United States, the "Four Freedoms" speech of Franklin Roosevelt, and the United Nations' Universal Declaration of Human Rights—should form some of the impermeable constructs for the educational practitioner/critical pedagogue. These should be used to deconstruct social justice issues and to create educational strategies to further their attainment. They should also form one of the foundations for building communities of learners throughout the school district. These communities of learners can become powerful forces in both shaping and fulfilling a district's educational mission.

CREATING COMMUNITIES OF LEARNERS BY BONDING THROUGH BOOKS

Most of us can probably remember times when in certain classes—elementary through graduate school—the subject matter was rich and through substantive dialogue students actually became classmates and colleagues. Learning communities of teachers and other school personnel can be created in a similar way. These communities can then tackle various issues, turn dull schools into exciting places of learning, and create the future rather than simply react to the present.

Educators rather than being school administrators can become educational leaders by providing space and time for substantive professional development designed to create such communities. This can be done through various activities: common field trips, sharing meals together, playing team sports, social gatherings, and others. One of the most powerful is by bonding through the common reading of thought-provoking books. In a school or district that is trying to build a greater awareness of racial sensitivity and social justice issues, books that advance that goal should be chosen. Five books in particular are proven winners leading to substantive dialogue sessions on racial and social justice issues:

- *The Bluest Eye* (Toni Morrison)[42]
- *The Lone Ranger and Tonto Fistfight in Heaven* (Sherman Alexie)[43]
- *Krik? Krak!* (Edwidge Danticat)[44]
- *Buck* (MK Asante)[45]
- *Autobiography of a Recovering Skinhead* (Frank Meeink and Jody Roy)[46]

Professional Development Using *The Bluest Eye*

Nobel Prize winner Toni Morrison's first novel, *The Bluest Eye*, is extremely powerful in depicting the dominance that one culture can have not only over another but also over individuals within the dominated culture. Her main character, Pecola, truly is one of the saddest, most despairing characters in all of American literature. She wants blue eyes so that she can be similar to Disney's Snow White or her idol Shirley Temple. This black girl can have neither. Not being particularly attractive, she is the butt of merciless taunts. Her miserable home life eventually leads to her being raped and impregnated by her father. Her friends plant marigold seeds believing that they will flower and her baby will live. There were no marigolds that year—and no baby. Pecola becomes disconnected from everything around her and convinces herself that at last she has blue eyes.

Deep and sensitive dialogue regarding the far-reaching and deep-seated effects that cultural dominance can have in creating racial hatred can be gained from several professional development sessions centered on this novel. It could be introduced to the group by viewing the beginning of the movie *The Littlest Rebel* (portions available on YouTube). Set in the pre–Civil War years, the film stars Shirley Temple and Bill "Bojangles" Robinson. The opening segment features Bojangles dancing at Virgie's (Shirley Temple's) birthday party and of her meeting with some black plantation children. When the black children stumble over the reading of birthday greetings to her, Virgie becomes very condescending while appearing to be overly sweet. Today this segment is usually seen as a shocking depiction of race relations. At the time it was not, being one of the top box office draws of 1935.

Dialogue on the film can go in many directions. Some of these are the portrayal of slaves as being of inferior intelligence, failure to reconcile the effects of slavery to this day, the supposed equality (and possibly equity) of all U.S. citizens as promised in our founding documents, and the acceptance or rejection of various historical depictions of race relations. This dialogue can lead to preparation for the next session with copies of *The Bluest Eye* given to all participants.

The next dialogue session should be planned so that there is sufficient time to read the novel and prepare an activity to share with the group. One activity that has proven effective is to draw a design (or prepare a Power-Point) that captures the essence of the novel. An example of a PowerPoint design prepared by the author is found in figure 4.1 Sharing different designs at the next dialogue session will open the group to rich conversations that should eventually lead to a consideration of race relations in the school or district. The group may decide on a particular design to eventually become part of a public display or possibly a mural arts project.

Two substantive things can happen as a result of these dialogue sessions. The first is that the administrator leading the dialogue, rather than administering someone else's ideas or mandates, will become the intellectual and affective educational leader of the group. The second is that the group actually changes and moves from being a "group" to becoming a community of learners. Another book that can produce similar effects is Sherman Alexie's *The Lone Ranger and Tonto Fistfight in Heaven*.

Professional Development Using *The Lone Ranger and Tonto Fistfight in Heaven*

Sherman Alexie, a Native American of mixed ancestry, is an award-winning author who spent his early years on the Spokane Indian Reservation. His series of short stories, *The Lone Ranger and Tonto Fistfight in Heaven*, appeared in 1993 and was eventually made into a movie, *Smoke Signals*, in 1998. It is a collection of short stories that is at times humorous and at others depressing. He captures the often sorrowful life that many Native Americans live in twenty-first-century America. A good example of one story is "The Only Traffic Signal on the Reservation Doesn't Flash Red Anymore," which depicts the futility of a traffic light when there is hardly any traffic—technology existing without a real purpose.

It is an example of the dialectic and tension that exists between pastoral and technological forces. In this respect it is reminiscent of Mark Twain's

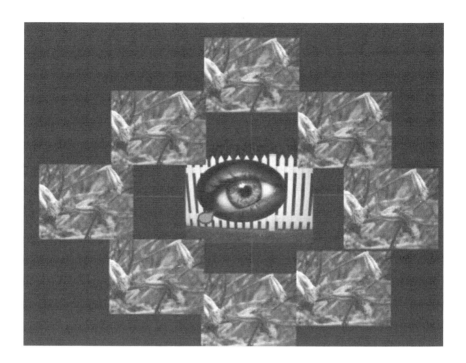

Figure 4.1. PowerPoint Design

Adventures of Huckleberry Finn when Huck Finn and Jim's floating revelry down the Mississippi is abruptly ended by the fiery crash of the forceful steamboat. Alexie's story also captures the tedium and dreariness of lives without purpose, a culture ripped from its roots, a people never really flourishing after being transplanted. Similar to *The Bluest Eye*, it raises serious questions regarding cultural dominance and the capacity of America to be truly multiethnic.

Rich dialogue sessions can be developed using this book. They could begin by viewing a portion of one of the many *Lone Ranger* TV episodes. One that has proven effective is 1954s "The Frightened Woman" (portions available on YouTube). Of particular interest is the way in which Tonto (a word that in Spanish means dumb or foolish) is treated: called an "injun," made to do menial labor, thought to have been a thief because that is what Indians did. Copies of the book should then be provided for all participants with them being asked to read one of the stories to share with the group at the next session.

The final session on this book could be a sharing of the various stories read by participants. The leader could then ask them to draw general themes from the various stories. The leader could relate the plight of the Native

Americans with those of the Aboriginal Australians who experienced a similar cultural takeover, relocation, and the reduction of their personhood to resemble curious animals in a zoo. The group could then find examples in their school or district in which similar cultural experiences may exist. As with the example of *The Bluest Eye*, a community of learners should emerge from these sessions with an administrator becoming an educational leader. Bonding through the book *Krik? Krak!* can have similar results.

Professional Development Using *Krik? Krak!*

Edwidge Danticat's *Krik? Krak!* is a powerful collection of nine short stories that portray the wretched conditions affecting most of Haiti's approximately eleven million people. Being the poorest nation in the western hemisphere, poverty and desolation are the norm rather than the exception.[47] The title is an invitation to become involved in storytelling (*Krik?*) to which you may respond yes (*Krak!*). One of these stories, "Children of the Sea," describes a desolate voyage of refugees leaving Haiti aboard a leaky boat that is overcrowded with those seeking a life free from poverty and persecution.

One of the passengers, fifteen-year-old Célianne, delivers a baby while at sea who is named Swiss after the army knife that was used to cut her umbilical cord. Swiss does not cry, and it soon becomes apparent that she is dead. Eventually Célianne throws her into the deep sea, following her moments later. Water keeps rising in the leaky boat until everyone throws all their possessions overboard, hoping to make the boat lighter. It does not work, and eventually they all become "Children of the Sea."

In 2010 the earth opened as a violent earthquake shook the poor island nation. Fragile buildings in the best of times quickly collapsed leaving an estimated three hundred thousand dead and hundreds of thousands homeless.[48] Medical teams from Harvard as well as other American hospitals and nations around the world responded.[49] One of those doctors was this author's daughter, who described the miserable conditions with doctors working under severe conditions often doing amputations without proper instruments and no anesthetic. This author saw the conditions firsthand on going to Haiti a few weeks after the earthquake with a team from Saint Joseph's University to ascertain what help, if any, we could bring to the ravaged school system. The devastation, the stench in the streets, the desperate faces of young and old alike searching for traces of help and hope are indelible memories that will last a lifetime.

Some generosity came from the U.S. government when it granted nearly sixty thousand Haitians Temporary Protected Status to come to the United States. The U.S. government announced in November 2017 that the extraordinary conditions that led to the granting of this status were over and that the Haitians had eighteen months to leave the United States.[50] Firsthand information confirms that tent cities still dot the Haitian countryside and poverty abounds everywhere.

Introducing dialogue sessions on *Krik? Krak!* could include some information on the poverty that exists in Haiti and the desperate conditions that so many are trying to escape. Numerous websites are available to provide this background information. A Google search of "Haiti poverty" will lead to many such as "Haiti Overview: World Bank Group," "Haiti Statistics," and "Haiti Statistics—Haiti Partners." An excellent book covering the history and some explanations for Haitian poverty is Tracy Kidder's *Mountains beyond Mountains*. Kidder documents the crusading work of Paul Farmer, Jennifer Furin, and other members of Partners in Health.

Dialogue participants could be given the book and asked to read one of the short stories for dialogue at the next session. Sharing stories at this session should reveal the realization that statistics and numbers are meaningless without imagining the faces and feeling the emotions of real people who suffer greatly. This conversation could eventually lead to a consideration of U.S. immigration policies and the "build a wall" mentality that denies the very essence of Emma Lazarus's "The New Colossus" sonnet on the Statue of Liberty, which contains these words:

> Give me your tired, your poor,
> Your huddled masses yearning to breathe free,
> The wretched refuse of your teeming shore.
> Send these, the homeless, tempest-tost to me,
> I lift my lamp beside the golden door! [51]

A good visual for this conversation would be artist John Tomac's February 3, 2017, cover of *The New Yorker* titled "Liberty's Flameout." It dramatically depicts a portion of the Statue of Liberty's right arm and hand holding aloft the torch that is now extinguished with spiraling smoke rising overhead.

Haitian immigrants are found in most of America's larger cities. There are often Haitian communities who would welcome an invitation to have someone come and speak to a gathering of teachers regarding immigration difficulties, poverty in Haiti, and other issues. This could be especially powerful if there are Haitian students among those in the school or district.

As with the previous examples, a community of learners should emerge from these sessions with an administrator becoming an educational leader. Additional important dialogue sessions could be held with a focus on two different books with similar themes: *Buck* and *Autobiography of a Recovering Skinhead.*

Professional Development Using *Buck* and
Autobiography of a Recovering Skinhead

These are two extremely powerful books that document the lives of two Philadelphia teens who for different reasons were alienated from traditional society and the schools that perpetuate it. It could be productive if they were considered together for back-to-back dialogue sessions.

Buck is the story of a Philadelphia teen, Malo Asante, whose parents worked hard to provide a private Friends school education for him. He rebels at the constraints of the school including the Meeting for Worship time, where he expressed one day that "I don't like this school because this school don't like me."[52] The head of the school forbids him to speak at Worship time again, which is only one of the many confrontations that they have. These grow more intense until he eventually leaves the school. His life spins out of control after his father abandons him and his mother is committed to the Philadelphia Psychiatric Center. He is drawn into the streets of North Philadelphia, which he calls "Killadelphia," and all of the drugs and crime that fill them. This is where he gets his real education.

After bouncing around for a while, he goes to Arizona to be near his brother Uzi, who is serving time in prison. He returns to Philadelphia and decides to return to school after many pleas from his mother. He enrolls in the private Crefeld School where he is encouraged to write. Stubbornness keeps him from doing so—until the blank page eventually reveals a passion in him to read and to write. This begins a stream of doing both that has not stopped. He is currently a professor at Morgan State, becoming tenured as the youngest in the history of the school.

Buck is an inspirational story that can start valuable conversations. Asante's style of writing is rich with poetry and hip-hop lyrics that give us a keyhole view of black culture. It makes us want to open the door wider.

A good introduction to sessions on *Buck* would be to view the Breakfast Club interview of Asante found on YouTube by googling "YouTube Asante interview breakfast club." Giving copies of the book to participants and asking them to read it would prepare for the next session. Past experiences using this book have found that it is a real page turner and that some individuals have said that they stayed up all night to finish it. Valuable dialogue will probably flow at the next session. It can open doors onto lives that are too often suppressed in America today. Connections can be made to youth in multiple school settings: black, white, suburban, urban, and rural.

Autobiography of a Recovering Skinhead is also about an alienated Philadelphia teen whose family life is extremely dysfunctional as it is filled with violent beatings and homelessness. He bounces in and out of Philadelphia schools being "expelled from at least two, maybe actually three schools in less than twelve months."[53] Eventually he finds the security and love that he seeks by shaving his head and becoming a neo-Nazi skinhead. Frank was involved in almost every type of viciousness associated with white supremacists and the KKK. He had a reputation as being one of the most brutal of the skinhead leaders in Pennsylvania.

After a stint in prison, he decided to turn his life around and eventually tells his story to Jody Roy, who wrote this book with him. He has been featured on many national programs such as NPR's Fresh Air and CNN. He makes appearances at colleges and universities throughout the country. Numerous sites, including some containing his speeches, are available on the internet by googling "Frank Meeink" or *Autobiography of a Recovering Skinhead.*

Preparation for dialogue sessions could include providing background on neo-Nazis and skinheads (see chapter 2 of this book). It might also be impressive to show one of his speeches. Caution: preview it first as the language is uncensored.

By comparing the two books, educators should realize it is not a question of being black or white that determines how a young student will turn out. Rather it is often poverty, weak family structures, and a lack of resources and compassion from both schools and society in general that create dysfunction.

SUMMARY

Five case studies have been presented that concern racial hatred and isolation: the Coatesville and the "Jena Six" episodes, "Dixie," Sister Henrietta's mission in an urban ghetto, and Camp Confidence. On the surface the first three began as relatively benign situations. The Coatesville and Jena Six nooses were considered by school authorities as an ignorant prank played by energetic teenagers who were not aware that symbolically hanging nooses represented a painful reminder of black lynchings in the Jim Crow South. "Dixie" was played by young band members. Neither they nor their band director were aware that the song could be hurtful to black members of the community because of its connection with slavery and the Confederacy's attempts to maintain it.

Racial hatred was not initially confronted in the Coatesville or Jena cases. In the Jena situation it exploded onto the national scene with demonstrations reminiscent of the civil rights movement of the 1960s. The "Dixie" situation was confronted before it became a crisis, and an increased sensitivity to racial prejudices was the result.

The other two case studies involved actions that need not have been taken. There was no outward pressure to build a bridge between the students in an all-white high school and Sister Henrietta's mission in one of Cleveland's worst ghettos. There was also no pressure to increase awareness of racial isolation and provide more opportunities for disadvantaged youth in the Owen J. Roberts school district through the Camp Confidence program. In both of these cases racial hatred was combated by increasing sensitivity to racial isolation and social justice issues. The theory and practice section of this chapter considers deconstruction and critical pedagogy as tools that can be helpful to educational leaders who want to combat racism. It also considers the concepts of permeable and impermeable constructs. Finally this chapter presents some specific books and suggests ways that they can be used as professional development materials to create communities of learners.

There are times that hatred comes from sources supposedly founded on sound religious and spiritual principles. One example of this is the intolerance that can come from the religious right. A case study of such an example is provided in the following chapter when a school superintendent and eventually the entire community confronted hatred and intolerance because a young Jewish woman, valedictorian of her class, did not want Christian prayer at the commencement where she was a featured speaker.

NOTES

1. "Black Doll Hung by Noose in High School Locker Room as Prank," *Associated Press*, October 11, 2017, https://nypost.com/2017/10/11/black-doll-hung-by-noose-in-high-school-locker-room-as-prank/ (accessed December 28, 2017).

2. "Incident More Hype than Reality," *Jena Times*, September 13, 2006, 1.

3. "Black Doll Hung by Noose in High School Locker Room as Prank."

4. Bill Sumrall, "Jena High Noose Incident Triggers Parental Protests," *Town Talk*, September 6, 2006.

5. "Incident More Hype than Reality."

6. Peter Whoriskey, "Thousands Protest Blacks' Treatment," *Washington Post*, September 21, 2007, http://www.washingtonpost.com/wp-dyn/content/article/2007/09/20/AR2007092000259_pf.html (accessed December 28, 2017).

7. Audie Cornish, "'Jena Six' Case Prompts Mass Demonstrations," *NPR*, September 20, 2007, http://www.npr.org/templates/story.php?storyLd=14574972 (accessed November 15, 2017).

8. "Coatesville Area School District: Hanging Doll Incident Insensitive, Not Hate Crime," 6 ABC Action News, WPVI TV, Philadelphia, October 11, 2017, http://6abc.com/education/coatesville-schools-doll-incident-insensitive-not-hate-crime/2517787/ (accessed December 18, 2017).

9. Jonathan Lai and Erin McCarthy, "Coatesville Students Walk Out in Protest over Racist Pumpkin Carvings," *Philadelphia Inquirer*, October 20, 2017, http://www.philly.com/philly/education/coatesville-high-school-protest-racism-carved-pumpkins-20171020.html (accessed December 18, 2017).

10. Walter Perez, "Pumpkins Carved with Racist Symbols Spark Outrage, Concern in Coatesville, Pa.," 6 ABC Action News, WPVI TV, Philadelphia, October 18, 2017, http://6abc.com/society/pumpkins-with-racist-symbols-spark-outrage-in-coatesville/2547874/ (accessed December 18, 2017).

11. "Incident More Hype than Reality," 2.

12. "Chronological Order of Events Concerning the 'Jena Six,'" *Jena Times*, www.thejenatimes.nte/home-page-graphics/home.html (accessed February 22, 2008). This quotation is taken from a publication that was prepared by the editor and staff of the *Jena Times* on an ongoing basis between August 30, 2006, and December 4, 2007. This site is no longer

functioning, and the "Chronological Order of Events Concerning the 'Jena Six,'" is no longer on the *Jena Times* homepage. The URL and article have been referenced several times by respected national news organizations such as the *New York Times* and the *Christian Science Monitor*. A hard copy of "Chronological Order of Events Concerning the 'Jena Six'" is in the author's files.

13. Lesli A. Maxwell, "'Jena Six': Case Study in Racial Tensions," *Education Week*, September 28, 2007, https://www.edweek.org/ew/articles/2007/10/03/06jena.h27.html (accessed December 30, 2017).

14. Bill Quigley, "Injustice in Jena as Nooses Hang from the 'White Tree,'" *Truthout*, http://truth-out.org/archive/component/k2/item/71606:bill-quigley--injustice-in-jena-as-nooses-hang-from-the-white-tree (accessed February 14, 2018).

15. "Chronological Order of Events Concerning the 'Jena Six.'"

16. Karen Long, "Methodists Crush Bid to Oust Wahoo," *Plain Dealer*, June 19, 1998.

17. Terrance Furin, "Chief Wahoo or Should I Wear My Hat or 'Dixie Revisited' (You Choose)," Owen J. Roberts website, fall 1998.

18. The *Encyclopedia of Cleveland History*, maintained by Case Western Reserve University, claims that 5 percent of the Hough area was nonwhite in 1950 and that in 1960 this number had grown to 74 percent. See http://ech.case.edu/ech-cgi/article.pl?id=H6 as well as http://ech.case.edu/ech-cgi/article.pl?id=HR3 for a brief history and description of the Hough area and the riots that began in July 1966. A thesis titled "The Hough Riots" written by Marc Lackritz provides a more detailed account of the riots. It can be found at http://www.clevelandmemory.org/hough/.

19. Albert Koklowsky, "A Voice from the Slums," *Catholic Universe Bulletin*, March 19, 1965.

20. Oral description provided by Sister Henreitta to Terrance Furin circa February 15, 1972.

21. Constitution of Caridad provided by an e-mail from Sister Mary Denis (smdm@srsofcharity.org), archivist for the Sisters of Charity of Saint Augustine to Terrance Furin, March 11, 2008.

22. Oral description provided by Sister Henreitta to Terrance Furin circa February 1972.

23. Sister Henrietta's goal for Famicos as provided in an e-mail from Sister Mary Denis (smdm@srsofcharity.org), archivist for the Sisters of Charity of Saint Augustine to Terrance Furin, March 11, 2008.

24. Peter Werwath, "Famicos Foundation—Helping Families Build Assets: Nonprofit Homeownership Program Profile," http://www.knowledgeplex.org/showdoc.html?id=163534.

25. Susan Weidner, "Summertime and the Schooling Is Easy," *Philadelphia Inquirer*, July 14, 1994, B1.

26. Ibid.

27. Ira Shor, *Empowering Education* (Chicago: University of Chicago Press, 1992), 15.

28. Ibid.

29. Ibid., 129.

30. Ibid., 129–30.

31. "Paradigm" is a word that has become part of most educators' vocabularies. It is usually used in discussions regarding the resistance to change encountered in reform efforts. It was originally a word popularized to describe scientific revolutions by Thomas Kuhn. His book *The Structure of Scientific Revolutions* (Chicago: University of Chicago Press, 1962) is the seminal work on defining paradigms and their effects in the scientific world. In this history and philosophy of science Kuhn defines paradigms as patterns or structures that science scholars establish over time that enable them to explain natural phenomena. Established paradigms become the standards or norms until anomalies in their ability to explain phenomena cause them to be replaced by new paradigms. These are scientific revolutions.

32. George Kelly, *A Theory of Personality: The Psychology of Personal Constructs* (New York: W. W. Norton and Company, 1963), 79.

33. William Faulkner, *The Sound and the Fury* (New York: Random House, 1956), 50–51.

34. Ibid.

35. *The Declaration of Independence*, second paragraph, July 4, 1776. http://www.ushistory.org/declaration/document/index.htm (accessed December 31, 2017).

36. The Bill of Rights from the *Constitution of the United States*, ratified December 15, 1791, http://www.law.cornell.edu/constitution/constitution.billofrights.html (accessed December 31, 2017).

37. Preamble, the Constitution of the United States, ratified May 29, 1790, http://www.law.cornell.edu/constitution/constitution.preamble.html (accessed December 31, 2017).

38. Franklin D. Roosevelt's Address to Congress, January 6, 1941, http://www.wwnorton.com/college/history/ralph/workbook/ralprs36b.htm (accessed December 31, 2017).

39. General Assembly of the United Nations, "Universal Declaration of Human Rights," December 1948, http://www.un.org/Overview/rights.html (accessed December 31, 2017).

40. Ibid.

41. Ibid.

42. Toni Morrison, *The Bluest Eye* (New York: Penguin Group, 1970).

43. Sherman Alexie, *The Lone Ranger and Tonto Fistfight in Heaven* (New York: Grove Press, 1993).

44. Edwidge Danticat, *Krik? Krak!* (New York: Vintage Books, 1991).

45. MK Asante, *Buck* (New York: Spiegel and Grau, 2013).

46. Frank Meeink and Jody Roy, *Autobiography of a Recovering Skinhead* (Portland, OR: Hawthorne Books, 2009).

47. "Haiti: The Challenges of Poverty Reduction," *World Bank*, http://web.worldbank.org/WBSITE/EXTERNAL/TOPICS/EXTPOVERTY/EXTPA/
0,,contentMDK:20207590~menuPK:435735~pagePK:148956~piPK:216618~theSitePK:430367,00.html (accessed January 3, 2018).

48. Richard Pallardy, "Haiti Earthquake of 2010," *Encyclopedia Britannica*, https://www.britannica.com/event/Haiti-earthquake-of-2010 (accessed January 2, 2018).

49. Elizabeth Cohen, "Slow Medical Care Is One More Thing for Quake Victims to Survive," *CNN*, January 17, 2010, http://www.cnn.com/2010/WORLD/americas/01/17/haiti.makeshift.hospitals/index.html (accessed January 2, 2018).

50. Karen DeYoung and Nick Miroff, "Trump Administration to End Provisional Residency Protection for 60,000 Haitians," *Washington Post*, https://www.washingtonpost.com/world/national-security/trump-administration-to-end-provisional-residency-protection-for-50000-haitians/2017/11/20/fa3fdd86-ce4a-11e7-9d3a-bcbe2af58c3a_story.html?utm_term=.e57a749d3a7a (accessed January 2, 2018).

51. Emma Lazarus, "The New Colossus," https://www.nps.gov/stli/learn/historyculture/colossus.htm (accessed January 3, 2018).

52. Asante, *Buck*, 34.

53. Meeink and Roy, *Autobiography of a Recovering Skinhead*, 103.

Chapter Five

Combating Hatred from the Religious Right

Anti-Christ
Satan
You will burn in hell[1]

Evangelical Christian fundamentalists[2] are often associated with promoting Christian prayer in public schools as prayer is seen as a conservative bulwark against liberal values that espouse tolerance and acceptance of a multitude of religious ideals. According to a Pew research study they number approximately 25.4 percent of those declaring religious affiliations in the United States.[3] Their political and social power is considerable. In the 2016 presidential election, approximately 80 percent voted for Donald Trump, who they saw as a more conservative candidate.[4] Some of them hurled abusive names and insults (this chapter's opening quotations) at me as superintendent of the Owen J. Roberts school district following the adoption of a new board policy that eliminated school prayer at all school events.

The insults were the result of a no-prayer policy adopted by the school board following a controversy over Christian prayer at the school's commencement. This controversy deepened into a crisis that severely divided the district. In the following school board election, four Christian fundamentalists won seats on a nine-member board after waging a "stealth" campaign that drew national attention.

Surviving the school prayer crisis was not easy. The first step in healing the deep wounds was to help the badly divided board move to common ground by following an unusual communication strategy based on some of Maxine Greene's ideas regarding aesthetics and Alexander Sidorkin's concepts of dialogue. Positive communications also proved to be a key in building bridges across the deep divisions that existed in the community. Building such bridges required many different communication approaches that were eventually successful in bringing the schools and the community together.

Many may assume that by the early 1990s the constitutional controversies regarding school prayer had been clarified by the U.S. Supreme Court. Key decisions in 1962 (*Engel v. Vitale*), 1963 (*Abington School District v. Schempp*), and 1971 (*Lemon v. Kurtzman*) made it apparent that the First Amendment's separation of church and state extended to the nation's public schools. The crisis at Owen J. Roberts demonstrated that there is often a great divide between decisions reached in Washington and local practice.

SCHOOL PRAYER CRISIS

Commencement Prayer Eliminated

She was a young Jewish woman in a public school district dominated by Christian fundamentalists. Nineteen-ninety was her senior year, and because she had the highest grade point average she was chosen as valedictorian of her class. Most people would never have known that she was Jewish had it not been for the required baccalaureate held prior to graduation. Following years of tradition, the service was heavy with Christian preaching. She and her family found the service not a source of pride but deeply offensive. Hoping to avoid similar distress at the commencement where she would speak three days later, the family approached the high school principal and asked whether Christian prayer was also on that program. When told that it was, they, with the aid of the American Civil Liberties Union (ACLU), filed suit in the Eastern District Federal Court and were granted a restraining order against prayer at the graduation ceremony. The community erupted with outrage.

One resident reportedly said, "It's terrible . . . you're taking one person's freedom of speech and stopping 200 others."[5] An editorial in the most popular of the local newspapers stated that the decision "smacks of fanaticism."[6] The editorial was accompanied by a cartoon depicting an ACLU lawyer as tolerant of abusive free speech in movies and rock music while attempting to muzzle a clergyman.[7]

This outcry set the stage for a conflict over freedom of religious expression that rocked this school district of nearly four thousand students. The situation was made worse by a transfer of power between two superintendents that left a leadership vacuum for the school board. Feeling pressure from the community, the board began preparing to fight the federal court's decision. As the new superintendent, I had other plans.

Taking a Stand

The outgoing superintendent's advice was to lie low on the prayer issue.[8] This did not seem to be an option as the U.S. Supreme Court decisions seemed to protect students' rights to individualized religious beliefs. They also recognized the important principle separating church and state in public schools. To fight the Christian fundamentalists by supporting the ACLU's ban on school prayer would be a daunting task. The administrative team— principals, assistant principals, and central office administrators—would need to be united. For this reason various members of that team researched school prayer rulings with their different professional organizations and to- gether developed a policy that eliminated prayer at all school-sponsored events.

The school board considered the policy before a hostile crowd of nearly five hundred citizens at a meeting prior to the start of the new school year. Philadelphia's major television stations, the *Philadelphia Inquirer*, and four local newspapers captured images of angry citizens demanding that the board defeat the proposed policy.

Leading the outcry was a representative from the Rutherford Institute who offered his services to fight the prayer ban all the way to the Supreme Court. After more than two hours of angry comments, the board voted unani- mously to approve the new policy. Chaos broke out in the auditorium. Above the pandemonium were heard shouts of "chickens," "yellow-bellies," and "you're running scared."[9]

The wrath of the Christian fundamentalists fell squarely on me as the new superintendent. I was stalked at my residence, had trash stolen, was called the Anti-Christ and Satan, received intimidating letters that warned of burning in hell, and was investigated by a private detective. My family, still residing in Ohio, was threatened as well. My youngest daughter, a high school freshman at the time, was questioned by authorities because someone anonymously reported me to children's services as a child abuser.

These hateful acts made it tempting to leave the district, but the issue was too important to leave. This obstinacy increased the anger and it became directed at the school board. One man's irate letter to a local newspaper captured the mood of many regarding the board when he wrote, "From their vote it's obvious that the current OJR School Board is comprised of a group of gutless wonders who are unresponsive to the wishes of the majority of taxpayers."[10]

Five of the nine school board seats were up for election the following year. Several Christian fundamentalists began a coordinated effort to capture a majority of these. Their campaign drew national attention and became a model across the country.

Wrath against the School Board: A Stealth Campaign

Four new school directors were elected following a political campaign that an article in *Education Week* cited as a "stealth campaign."[11] This term captured the political strategy used by a team of Christian fundamentalists who on the surface ran as separate individuals. It was only after the election that a national organization known as the National Association of Christian Educators/Citizens for Excellence in Education (often referred to simply as CEE) proclaimed that a "Tremendous Victory in School Board Race" had occurred in this district and that the individual winners had in reality run as a team.[12]

CEE's *Education Newsline*, sent to the organization's 868 chapters, declared the victory in this local school board election as "nothing short of a miracle."[13] In this same newsletter, one of the newly elected local school directors outlined the plan that the Christian fundamentalist team had followed. Key elements explained in this plan included these tactics:

- The team found a committed Christian who was willing to take the reins of managing the campaign and did not make any decisions unless they were cleared through him.
- The team emphasized running individually and not as a slate yet met regularly to plan campaign strategies.
- A few days before the election the team advertised that each individual was supported by an amorphous committee, in this case called the Citizens for Responsive Education, which would help voters link the names together.
- The week before the election each candidate called voter lists, scheduled cottage prayer meetings, and on the eve of the election held a large prayer rally for supporters.[14]

The plan worked. It is little wonder that Robert Simonds, head of CEE, was boastful. He wrote in a *President's Report* soon after the election that "we have meticulously followed God's plan and His biblical principles . . . to redeem America's children from the clutches of atheism, immorality and psychological brainwashing."[15]

The board was now badly divided. This made it difficult if not impossible for the board/administrative team to provide leadership for the school district. The community itself was also deeply divided. Hatred based on intolerance had turned into vengeance.

Combating the Crisis: Dialoguing Great Literature over Breakfast

Quick and decisive actions were needed if there was any hope of creating an atmosphere in which the board and administration could find common ground for working together. This was a necessary first step toward bridging the deep divisions within the community. To this end the administrative leadership team scheduled a series of orientation meetings over the next several months that were designed to deal with topics such as school finance, curriculum, personnel procedures, policy development, and other matters. The first of these meetings would be the most important as it would be the initial meeting between new and former board members.

This meeting was not planned to deal with routine matters or school board procedures. It was designed to begin a conversation that would lead to the board becoming a community of learners where the inherent equality and dignity of each person would be acknowledged. Ernest Hemingway, the literary giant, helped begin this conversation. His classic, *The Old Man and the Sea*, was the focus for the first meeting, a dialogue session, scheduled for 8:00 a.m. on a cold and snowy Saturday morning in January.

The dialogue session started with a candlelight breakfast for nine board members and three central office administrators. In preparation for the session each participant was given a copy of Ernest Hemingway's 1952 novel *The Old Man and the Sea*. This book by the Nobel Prize–winning author was chosen because it was not only a quick read but was also profoundly simple and at the same time very deep. Everyone was asked to read it beforehand, and they all did arrive with books in hand.

The breakfast, candles, and soft background music from *Out of Africa* proved to be somewhat of an icebreaker even though individuals clustered together in groupings with known colleagues. This soon changed when everyone assembled around a large table and began a conversation by considering Hemingway's use of color in the novel.

The reflection on color was begun by reading a quotation from the novel in which Hemingway described the first time that the old man, Santiago, saw the giant fish that he caught on his third day far out at sea. Hemingway painted with vivid colors this way: "He was bright in the sun and his head and back were dark purple and in the sun the stripes on his sides showed wide and a light lavender."[16] Following that reading everyone was asked to reflect privately on what color they would choose to describe the entire novel.

After several minutes each person presented a color and explained what it meant to him or her. Dialogue between supposed adversaries began. There could be no right or wrong answers, and individuals learned much about each other by responding to the question.

Following this activity, individuals began to focus on three themes in the novel: heroism, man and nature (harmony or conflict), and spiritual symbolisms. Individuals were assigned one of the themes, and after some quiet time, during which they sought ideas from the novel relative to their theme, three groups were formed. The groupings were prearranged to contain new and former board members plus an administrator who served as a facilitator. Individuals shared their thoughts and findings with other members of their group for about thirty minutes. They then chose a spokesperson to summarize the group's dialogue for everyone else.

While each group presented interesting commentaries, the most memorable came from the spiritual symbolism group. The spokesperson for this group was the minister who was the person chosen to give the invocation at the notorious commencement. Now, as one of the newly elected board members, he presented many examples of spiritual symbols from the novel.

One of these was the importance of the number three. For example, Santiago (Spanish for Saint James) had to endure three nights before hooking the marlin. He compared this with the New Testament importance of the number three as in Jesus's resurrection on the third day and the theological significance of the trinity. Other illustrations included Santiago's occupation as a fisherman, his loneliness at being abandoned, and his frequent prayers.

The most poignant of the examples was the board member's comparison of the crucifixion of Jesus with the scene near the end of the novel in which Hemingway described Santiago falling several times while climbing a hill to his shack with the mast of the skiff across his shoulders. This scene unfolded with a background of the white bones of the marlin's skeleton still attached to the skiff, bobbing in the water—a reminder of the prophet Ezekiel's description of the valley of dry bones.

This board member spoke with deep feelings that charged the atmosphere in the room for several silent moments after he finished speaking. Everyone felt deeply moved. It was truly a transcendent experience that testified to the power of dialogue.

In summarizing the morning's experiences, participants came to realize that they had come together and had acted as a community of learners. On the blackboard each board member was asked to list behaviors that were considered fair or acceptable to be a member of such a community of learners. This is a summary of their list of acceptable behaviors:

- attendance
- preparation
- participation
- open-mindedness
- a willingness to share both thoughts and feelings
- being a good listener

- respecting the views of others
- focusing on ideas rather than individuals
- constructive criticism
- objectivity
- common courtesy
- honesty
- a willingness to accept majority views
- being up front
- enthusiasm

Each person was asked to review the list and object if there was anything with which they could not agree. Everyone accepted the list and agreed that it would become a type of contract for future interactions. Even though there were times over the next few years that the board and central office administrators needed to review the agreed-upon behaviors, it proved to be a remarkably durable accord.

During the six months following *The Old Man and the Sea* session the board met with key administrators seventeen times beyond their regularly scheduled public meetings for in-service sessions that dealt with practical matters such as school board policies and procedures. These sessions proved to be important as they strengthened the relationships that had begun during the Saturday dialogue session. As important as these sessions were, the most important meeting was their initial encounter when open communications based on honest dialogue helped nine board members and central office administrators find common ground where they could respect each other and begin working together for the benefit of the district's students.

The ideas of two prominent educational theorists are demonstrated in that Saturday dialogue session. One of these is Maxine Greene and her thoughts regarding aesthetics. The other is Alexander Sidorkin and his concepts of dialogue.

THEORY AND PRACTICE: AESTHETIC EXPERIENCES AND AUTHENTIC DIALOGUE

Maxine Greene and Learning through Aesthetic Experiences

Maxine Greene, former professor at Columbia University's Teachers College, is a leading educational theorist regarding the importance of aesthetic experiences. She was a pupil of John Dewey's and, similar to him, advocated the strong position that aesthetics should hold in a progressive educational philosophy.

Greene has written numerous books that make known her passion regarding the potential that various art forms have in creating new perspectives and enriched learning experiences. In *Variations on a Blue Guitar* she wrote that following an aesthetic encounter "we experience a sense of surprise often-times, an acute sense that things may look otherwise, feel otherwise, *be* otherwise than we have assumed—and suddenly the world seems new, with possibilities still to be explored."[17]

Gaining new perspectives can bring people together and help them dream. Maxine Greene believes that aesthetic experiences can make this happen more readily. She wrote in *Landscapes for Learning*, "I would want to see one or another art form taught in all pedagogical contexts, because of the way in which aesthetic experiences provide a ground for the questioning that launches sense-making and the understanding of what it is to exist in a world."[18]

Ernest Hemingway's powerful writing caused the participants to "experi-ence a sense of surprise"[19] and have an encounter with each other in which they looked at things differently and became something other than they had assumed prior to the session. The dialogue session helped them further by "launch[ing] sense-making and the understanding of what it [was] to exist in a world."[20] Though it was probably not his intended purpose, Ernest Hem-ingway helped these diverse individuals find common ground on which they began to build a community of learners.

Alexander Sidorkin's thoughts concerning dialogue also provide a theo-retical understanding to *The Old Man and the Sea* session. Sidorkin offers insights into the term "dialogue" that has become a popular expression among managers in both education and the corporate world. Many of these managers see dialogue as a process to gain support for various proposals or to build coalitions for organizational goals. Used in these ways dialogue is oftentimes not free flowing or democratic but instead represents a process to rubber stamp preconceived views. A better word to use in these cases would be "discussion," a percussive term that differentiates it from more authentic dialogue.

Raymond Horn, a prominent educational leadership theorist formerly at Saint Joseph's University in Philadelphia, probed deeply into the meaning of the term "dialogue" in his article "Differing Perspectives on the Magic of Dialogue: Implications for a Scholar-Practitioner Leader" that appeared in a 2002 issue of *Scholar Practitioner Quarterly*. His work is especially impor-tant in distinguishing the difference between a systems approach to dialogue often used in an organizational context and dialogue founded on true demo-cratic principles.

Horn described the importance of a leader being a scholar-practitioner and connected such a leader with the importance of democratic dialogue. He wrote that "scholar-practitioner leaders are active agents in human affairs, and therefore recognize the primacy of conversation, especially when agree-ment needs to be reached among groups with divergent positions."[21]

After establishing the importance of dialogue for scholar practitioners, Horn presents four different perspectives of dialogue through a review of books by Elizabeth Ellsworth (*Teaching Positions: Difference, Pedagogy, and the Power of Address*), William Isaacs (*Dialogue and the Art of Thinking Together*), Daniel Yankelovich (*The Magic of Dialogue: Transforming Conflict into Cooperation*), and Alexander Sidorkin (*Beyond Discourse: Education, the Self, and Dialogue*).

Horn contends that two of these authors, Isaacs and Yankelovich, develop dialogue theories in the context of organizational management systems. Both of these see dialogue as important in leading to anticipated understandings. This approach is not essentially democratic, and Horn criticizes it this way: "However, in both cases, the anticipated understanding will not significantly recognize the inherent difference between the participants, and will pressure some participants to suppress their ideas and feelings in order to promote dialogic coherence and continuity."[22]

Horn finds support for his belief regarding such management systems approaches in Elizabeth Ellsworth's writing. According to him she supports his view as she sees most dialogues as attempts to impose controlling values, especially those of the leader who has arranged for the dialogue session. He finds similar support from Alexander Sidorkin whose views on dialogue are based on core democratic values. It is Sidorkin's views that resonate most completely with the Saturday dialogue session on Hemingway's *The Old Man and the Sea*.

Sidorkin's concept of dialogue is far more attuned with human rather than organizational qualities. He wrote that "we are human in the fullest sense when we engage in dialogue."[23] He contends further that dialogue is not a process or means to accomplish some other aim. It by itself is the goal. He stated this concept as follows: "Dialogue is an end in itself, the very essence of human existence."[24] This conception of dialogue requires a democratic context in which all beings are viewed with inherent equality and dignity. Within such a context it is possible to relate fully with another human being. When this relationship occurs, important dialogue happens. This relationship, in Sidorkin's words, "takes you completely out of your regular life."[25]

A greater understanding of the dynamics of the Saturday dialogue session emerges when we couple Sidorkin's views of dialogue with Maxine Greene's ideas regarding the importance of aesthetic experiences. Creating dialogue itself was the goal of the Saturday session, and Hemingway's novel proved to be an effective art form through which to establish it within a democratic context. Open communications and honest dialogue helped move perceived adversaries onto common ground where they respected the genuine importance of each other as human beings.

Open communications also proved to be keys in building bridges across the deep divisions that had opened in the community as a result of the school prayer controversy. One of the most important of these communications efforts began with development of a district mission statement—a statement that captured the community's beliefs, hopes, and dreams for its students. Various open communications initiatives were also used to build positive relationships with specific constituencies in the community that included religious groups, civic organizations, and senior citizens.

USING POSITIVE COMMUNICATIONS TO BUILD BRIDGES IN A DIVIDED COMMUNITY

Developing a District Mission Statement: Let's Build a Lighthouse

The first step in effective strategic planning is for educational leaders to facilitate the development of a mission statement that truly belongs to the community. Once developed, this statement should be the critical standard for policy development, curriculum design, personnel procedures, financial decisions, and other district activities.

The process to design a mission statement for the Owen J. Roberts school district was called "Mission 21." It was planned to be a propelling force to take the district well into the twenty-first century. A lighthouse became the symbol to characterize the statement's importance in guiding the actions of the district. The lighthouse base and beacons were created by input from the district's students, parents, teachers, support staff members, and citizens. This input began with a widely distributed questionnaire that asked four basic questions:

- What purpose do you think education has in our democratic society?
- What do you think is the most important skill for students to have by the time they graduate from high school?
- What do you think is the most important value or attitude for students to have by the time they graduate from high school?
- If you could improve one thing about the curriculum of the school district, what would that be?

More than 650 students, recent graduates, staff members, and community residents responded to the survey. These responses were reviewed, categorized, and used to write a mission statement that reflected this input. The statement recognized the importance of developing both cognitive learning (skills and knowledge acquisition) as well as attitudes (values and human relations concepts).

The mission statement was synthesized into a graphic representation of a lighthouse. The foundation consisted of educational processes important across all skill areas: problem solving, analytical and creative thinking, and study skills. The main body of the lighthouse included the curricular areas of communications, math, social studies, science, fine arts, physical education, health, and various vocational areas. The lighthouse beacons represented the important values in the statement: positive self-esteem, personal responsibility, honesty and integrity, social and environmental responsibility, respect and concern for others, and positive attitudes. [26] Pictured in figure 5.1 is the representation of the lighthouse that was sent to Owen J. Roberts's staff and community.

The school board adopted the new mission statement on April 8, 1991. Both the statement and the process to develop it were well accepted and considered important. An editorial written the week prior to the board's adoption of the statement reflected the changed tone of the community when it stated,

> No district can reach any goals unless they are firmly understood and shared by all its members. If Owen J. Roberts can reach a consensus on a philosophy, and take it seriously, the philosophy can serve as a yardstick to evaluate programs and set priorities. [27]

This was an important endorsement as this same newspaper had been highly critical of the board's decision to eliminate prayer from school-sponsored events seven months earlier. Focusing on education and designing a mission statement in this manner did, indeed, build an important bridge across the school prayer divide. Other bridges were built by reaching out to religious organizations.

Reaching Out to Religious Organizations

There was a religious association in the Owen J. Roberts school district known as the Ministerium whose membership included most of the pastors, ministers, and priests who had congregations within the district. This group of approximately twenty religious leaders met monthly and sponsored some coordinated activities.

One of these was an annual Crop Walk that involved participants securing sponsors to donate various amounts of money for them to walk several miles on a Sunday afternoon. The money was used to support area food banks and provide food baskets to needy families. After discussing various ways to improve relationships with community churches, district administrators decided that it would be a good idea to become involved with the Crop Walk. They discussed the idea with members of the Ministerium who enthusiastically welcomed their support. The idea was shared with middle and high school teachers and students. It was strongly accepted.

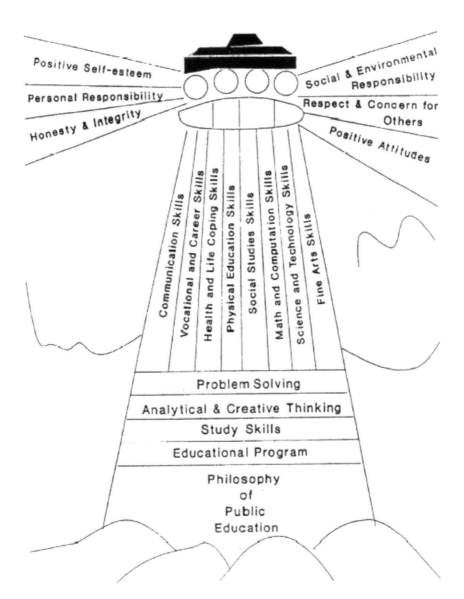

Figure 5.1.   The Representation of the Lighthouse

The first year that the school district supported the event, participation increased from approximately 150 crop walkers to more than 600. The walk began and ended in a local park where members of the Ministerium served light refreshments to the sounds of upbeat music. The atmosphere was festive as students, teachers, and educational leaders mixed freely with clergy members and citizens of the community. Thousands of dollars were raised to benefit needy individuals and families.

The Crop Walk opened the door for ongoing conversations between members of the clergy and various school district personnel. School administrators were invited to go to different meetings at various churches and explain the rationale for the no prayer policy. These were important conversations that seemed to alleviate some of the anger over the "no prayer in school" policy. Positive communications led to other cooperative efforts with Ministerium members including support of the Salvation Army's "Angels" gift-gathering event, "Caring and Sharing" projects that collected items for needy families, and the establishment of an after-school Bible club. In addition to these activities with religious organizations, students, teachers, administrators, and board members also became engaged with projects sponsored by various civic organizations in the district.

Reaching Out to Civic Organizations

The four most active civic organizations in the Owen J. Roberts school district during the time of the prayer controversy were the Lions Club, the Kiwanis club, a local arts organization known as Friends of the Arts, and the Tri County Chamber of Commerce, a chamber serving parts of Berks, Chester, and Montgomery counties. District administrators and school board members joined these organizations and helped them with various projects.

One involved supporting an annual pancake breakfast for the Lions that was coupled with a free car wash run by members of the high school track teams. Other examples included helping the Kiwanis club organize a Circle K club at the high school and supporting the Friends of the Arts annual craft show and sale that was held at the district's middle school. As important as these activities were, none was as significant as the district's involvement with the Tri County Chamber of Commerce and the American Cancer Society's "Relay for Life."

The Tri County Chamber of Commerce, centered in Pottstown, Pennsylvania, is the local sponsor for the American Cancer Society's "Relay for Life." This is both a charitable and community-building event that raises money for the American Cancer Society by having teams of participants walk a track continuously for twenty-four hours. It is an engaging activity as teams set up tents for sleeping, vendors sell refreshments, and various groups provide entertainment for two days and one night. The most inspirational part of the relay occurs at dusk when thousands of luminaries provided by cancer survivors are lit and survivors as well as others walk the track late into the night.

Until 1998 the Tri County Chamber of Commerce had held the relay at a private school in Pottstown. Because of parking limitations and other considerations, the chamber sought a different place to hold the event. The president of the chamber approached members of the school district's administration and requested to use the school district's central campus that contained the athletic facilities and ample parking for thousands of people.

District officials recognized an opportunity to build positive community relations and approved the request. Students and district personnel became heavily involved at the next year's relay. Schools sponsored many teams, student performing groups provided entertainment, and district maintenance as well as security personnel supplied essential services. Thousands of people from the district and surrounding communities attended the relay and for several days Owen J. Roberts was the center of the tri-county area. This was an amazing event, a catalyst for community building, that brought together individuals from diverse backgrounds to support a worthy cause.

Relays continued to be held for several years at the same site. Hundreds of thousands of dollars were raised and donated to the American Cancer Society. The success of these relays symbolized in a dramatic way the distance the district had come since intolerance and hatred had sharply divided it during the prayer controversy a few years earlier.

In addition to reaching out to religious and civic organizations, Owen J. Roberts administrators, teachers, and students began communicating in a significant way with the district's senior citizens. At the time of the prayer crisis only 27 percent of the district's residents had children of school age, and many senior citizens had complained for years that their taxes were high and that they received little in return for paying them. The school prayer issue was the last straw for some of them, and they were among the most vocal in protesting the board's policy banning it.

Reaching Out to Senior Citizens

Following the prayer controversy members of the Owen J. Roberts school board and administration took several steps to become more engaged with the community. Regular school board meetings were moved from a small board room on the central campus to large meeting spaces at various schools throughout the district. Time was added to board agendas for general community comments on unscheduled topics. Regular communications forums were scheduled with no preset agendas. These forums were very informal and resembled community coffee klatches in which any topic could be raised and discussed. It was during one of these that school leaders learned from senior citizens that they would like to have a senior center opened if space was available in one of the schools.

One of the district's elementary schools had been remodeled recently, and a room was available. It became a popular senior citizen center that was used for social activities as well as a place where tax services and counseling on various topics such as Medicare were provided. School administrators would often drop by the center for informal visits. During one of these the idea for a "Senior Prom" was born.

The "Senior Prom" was an after school dance for senior citizens and elementary school students. It began at one school and was quickly adopted by others. Weeks before the event senior citizens, especially those with no grandchildren in the area, were identified and paired with elementary school students. Students and seniors began corresponding with each other so that they would not be strangers on the afternoon of the prom.

The prom itself was an amazing event. School multipurpose rooms were transformed into festive ballrooms. Upon arrival seniors met their students and were presented with corsages and boutonnieres before being escorted through a balloon archway into the ballroom. Tables were decorated with student artwork and held a variety of light refreshments. Formal pictures were taken of the seniors and their newfound elementary-aged friends. DJs played oldie tunes that fascinated both generations. Many students and seniors danced together or sat and talked until the prom ended nearly two hours later.

For many the newly formed relationships did not end with the prom. Several seniors volunteered in the schools where they became library and classroom aides. They worked with students in numerous other ways such as sharing skills with crafts, music, and gardening. Such intergenerational associations were important in building positive relationships at a time when many seniors were alone and students were without grandparents nearby.

These various outreach initiatives with the community's religious leaders, civic organizations, and senior citizens demonstrated the power that positive communications had in closing the divide between the community and the schools that had been opened by the controversy over school prayer. These were not the only positive communications plans that took place at this time.

There was a concerted effort to improve general public relations and associations with members of the media. These included regular meetings with newspaper editorial boards to explain district happenings, publication of a school district newsletter and calendar, hosting a regular call-in radio show, and meetings with local realtors to distribute information packets and answer questions regarding the school district.

As important as all of the outreach and public relations efforts were in healing the deep wounds created by the school prayer crisis, it appears in retrospect that none of them would have been possible without the initial Saturday dialogue session that created an atmosphere and expectation for open and democratic communications. These communications respected the dignity and value of each human being. They enabled not only the school board but many important constituencies within the district itself to bridge the divides and rise above the intolerance and hatred that were revealed in the prayer crisis.

SUMMARY

A commencement prayer controversy badly divided the Owen J. Roberts community following the adoption of a new school board policy that eliminated prayer at all school events. This controversy deepened into a crisis that severely divided the district following a school board election in which four Christian fundamentalists won seats on a nine-member board after waging a "stealth" campaign that drew national attention.

The election resulted in a badly divided board that eventually found common ground following an unusual communication strategy based on some of Maxine Greene's ideas regarding aesthetics and Alexander Sidorkin's concepts of dialogue. Positive communications also proved to be a key in building bridges across the deep divisions that existed in the community. Building such bridges required many different communication approaches that were eventually successful in bringing the schools and the community together.

Several of the district's educational leaders were important catalysts in developing these positive communications. In doing this, they exhibited some of the behaviors consistent with the term "transformational leadership" that has been identified by important scholars who have studied the dynamics of leadership. Transformational leadership seems to be a critical factor in combating hatred and increasing awareness of social justice for everyone. For this reason it is the focus of the next chapter.

NOTES

1. These were some of the phrases hurled at me as superintendent of the Owen J. Roberts school district when we confronted religious intolerance over school prayer. They came in the form of letters and notes that I have in a personal file.

2. The difference between evangelicals and Christian fundamentalists is that evangelicals are often defined as the umbrella group with Christian fundamentalists being a smaller subgroup. For purpose of this chapter the distinctions are not made as it was unclear whether the groups opposing school prayer were evangelicals or fundamentalists. For consistency the term "Christian fundamentalist(s)" will be used.

3. "Religious Landscape Study," Pew Research Center, 2015, http://www.pewforum.org/religious-landscape-study/ (accessed January 4, 2018).

4. Sarah Puliam Bailey, "White Evangelicals Voted Overwhelmingly for Donald Trump, Exit Polls Show," *The Washington Post*, November 9, 2016, https://www.washingtonpost.com/news/acts-of-faith/wp/2016/11/09/exit-polls-show-white-evangelicals-voted-overwhelmingly-for-donald-trump/?utm_term=.248bd6455be8 (accessed January 4, 2018).

5. Debra Noell, "At OJR the Graduates Didn't Have a Prayer," *The Mercury*, June 14, 1990, 8.

6. Editorial, "U.S. Supreme Court Attempts to Deny Our Spiritual Heritage," *The Mercury*, June 24, 1990, A10.

7. Ibid.

8. Roy Claypool and Terrance Furin, personal communication, June 15, 1990.

9. Derrick Gray, "OJR Passes Prayer Ban," *The Mercury*, August 28, 1990, 1.

10. Michael Moyer, letter to the editor, *The Mercury*, September 5, 1990, 6.

11. Ann Bradley, "Christian Activists Set Their Sights on School Board Seats," *Education Week*, October 7, 1992, 1, 16.

12. The National Association of Christian Educators/Citizens for Excellence in Education (CEE) was located in Costa Mesa, California. Robert Simonds, president of the organization, stated in the December 1991 *President's Report* that the organization had a national network of 868 chapters. In 2006 he claimed that CEE had more than 1,680 chapters representing more than 350,000 active parents.

13. "Tremendous Victory in School Board Race," *Education Newsline*, September/October 1992 (Costa Mesa, CA: National Association of Christian Educators/Citizens for Excellence in Education), 1–4.

14. Ibid.

15. Robert Simonds, *President's Report* (Costa Mesa, CA: National Association of Christian Educators/Citizens for Excellence in Education, December 1991).

16. Ernest Hemingway, *The Old Man and the Sea* (New York: Macmillan Publishing, 1952), 62.

17. Maxine Greene, *Variations on a Blue Guitar* (New York: Teachers College Press, 2001), 116.

18. Maxine Greene, *Landscapes for Learning* (New York: Teachers College Press, 1978), 166.

19. Maxine Greene, *Variations*, 116

20. Maxine Greene, *Landscapes*, 166.

21. Raymond Horn, "Differing Perspectives on the Magic of Dialogue: Implications for Scholar-Practitioner Leader," *Scholar Practitioner Quarterly* 1, no. 2 (2002): 84.

22. Ibid., 100.

23. Alexander Sidorkin, *Beyond Discourse: Education, the Self, and Dialogue* (Albany: State University of New York Press, 1999), 4.

24. Ibid., 14.

25. Ibid., 18.

26. Owen J. Roberts School District Mission Statement, adopted April 8, 1991.

27. Editorial, "Owen J. Roberts School District Develops Educational Philosophy," *The Mercury*, March 21, 1991, 6.

Chapter Six

Transformational Educational Leaders

Creating Communities That Changed Worlds

The transactional leader function[s] as a broker. [1]

But to transform something . . . is to cause a metamorphosis in form or structure, a change in the very condition or nature of a thing . . . radical change in outward form or inner character. [2]

TRANSFORMATIONAL LEADERSHIP

Transformational leadership is an elusive concept. Even though it is difficult to provide a precise definition, we usually know when we are engaged with transformational leaders. These are the times when our intellects are buzzing with fresh ideas fueled with new perspectives; times when our emotions are bursting and carry us to places we have not been before. These are the times when individual identities are lost in a true democratic community, times when leaders and followers are often indistinct as they grow together fueled by a common mission toward a common vision.

Educational leaders who are successful in combating hatred on a continuing basis are those who embrace the central concepts of transformational leadership: community, mission, and vision. These leaders build communities of believers who share a common social justice mission and work to manifest it through a particular vision. Such a vision grows from the mission and sometimes it is provided by an inspired leader and embraced by the community. Sometimes it grows from members of the community and is embraced by the leader. In either event, when working toward the common vision inspired by the community's mission, a metamorphosis often takes place, and the community moves to a higher plane, a transcendent level, together.

Those seeking to become transformational educational leaders often seek some magic formula that can be easily replicated. There is no such formula. To understand the concept of transformational leadership better, individuals can examine several studies beginning with James MacGregor Burns's 1978 Pulitzer Prize–winning book *Leadership* in which he popularizes the terms "transforming" or "transformational leadership." In this book and its 2003 companion, *Transforming Leadership*, he analyzed several major historical world figures and drew from them qualities, situations, and actions that he felt distinguished them as transformational ones.

Burns's clearest definition of transformational leadership occurs when he contrasts it with transactional leadership. He defines transactional leadership as political give and take in which leaders negotiate from different power positions and trade favors to accomplish objectives.[3] By contrast, transformational leadership can be far more significant and cause fundamental changes that involve a metamorphosis in form or structure.[4] He described transformational leaders as those who are able to inspire others to help accomplish such changes. He ends *Leadership* by writing about Woodrow Wilson as follows: "Woodrow Wilson called for leaders who, by boldly interpreting the nation's conscience, could lift a people out of their everyday selves. That people can be lifted *into* their better selves is the secret of transforming leadership."[5]

Several scholars, such as Bernard Bass and Kenneth Leithwood, have added to Burns's seminal work and advanced our understanding of the concept.[6] Rather than examine the works of Burns, Bass, Leithwood, and others in greater detail, let us follow a different approach, one similar to that employed by Burns, and examine case studies of five educators in a variety of positions and settings who can be defined as transformational educational leaders. Each of these individuals fused the concepts of community, mission, and vision and caused a metamorphosis in their particular situation. Each of the communities that they created was based on a mission of social justice that was effective in combating the ignorance, indifference, or prejudice that oftentimes is the foundation for hatred. It is hoped that educational leaders—especially those who wish to combat hatred, advance social justice, and expand equity—can draw both information and inspiration from these studies so that they might be enabled to become transformational educational leaders.

No one will ever know how much hatred was dispelled or how much social justice and equity were enhanced by the heroic actions of the transformational educational leaders that will be described in this chapter. It surely was considerable. Their examples can serve as inspirations to educational leaders who daily face situations that are or have the potential of becoming hate filled. To confront the conditions that lead to hatred or the hatred itself demands courage and sensitivity. America and the world desperately need such courageous and sensitive educational leaders—leaders who are truly transformational.

The first case study is of a gifted high school teacher, a person of great intellect and sensitivity to social justice issues, who became the secondary social studies coordinator for a large suburban school district.[7] He was dissatisfied with an outdated and, as he often called it, "pedestrian" social studies curriculum. He believed that it failed to address the most crucial issues facing the world: issues of greed and hatred that if ignored could mean the elimination of our species.

He formed a community of learners consisting of approximately seventy-five teachers who developed a philosophy of social studies education that led to a curriculum that engaged students in examining the four most serious issues facing the world. This community of learners totally redesigned the grades 7 to 12 social studies curriculum to not only educate students regarding critical problems but also to reflect more completely key social justice ideals that should be taught in a democracy's schools.

The second case study is of a nun who also built a community of learners that designed a philosophy of education that drove critical decisions.[8] The development of this philosophy was for an all-women's Catholic high school. As the school principal, the nun faced the exciting task of building a new school to replace an antiquated one that was literally falling down. Her initial meeting with the chosen architect ended in disaster.

He wanted to know the philosophy and the curriculum of the new school so that he could design a building that would flow from them. The principal told him that the philosophy and curriculum were the standard ones found in most Cleveland area Catholic high schools. This was not a sufficient answer for the architect. He wanted it to be their philosophy and their curriculum. Recognizing an unusual creative moment, the principal delayed the construction plans for an additional year during which she formed a community of nuns, teachers, alumni, students, and parents in designing an innovative philosophy and curriculum that were based on high intellectual achievement and Catholic social justice ideals.

The third case study is of a school district superintendent who believed so strongly in the values of American public education that he worked against great odds to create a community of advocates who campaigned tirelessly to pass a badly needed bond issue.[9] This was required to provide a quality education for all students in a small suburban school district. This district's citizens had refused time and again to vote for additional bonds to pay for additional school facilities. This forced some students to attend school half-time, which gave them a second-class education.

The fourth case study is of a foreign educator—a Jesuit teacher in Chile.[10] He was a man who made both his Christian values and his pedagogical principles the center of his life. His 1935 doctoral dissertation compared John Dewey's educational philosophy with Catholic doctrine. After completing his studies in Belgium, he returned to Chile where he experienced a profound event that caused him to create a public pedagogy that in many ways turned the entire country into a Dewey-like classroom.

He formed a community of believers who helped him achieve his vision of founding a charity for homeless people that has become one of the largest and most beneficial in Latin America. He was a true transformational leader whose lifetime of service to others was recognized by the Catholic Church when he was canonized as a saint in 2005.

The fifth case study is of a phenomenal woman whose deep-seated beliefs in social justice, which she believed could be achieved through art forms, enabled her to found the mural arts project in Philadelphia (Mural Arts Philadelphia).[11] Today Philadelphia is considered the world's number one city for mural arts. Graffiti has turned into elaborate art forms that not only adorn buildings but also give pride and life to communities that they help create and stabilize. Golden's is an example of public pedagogy that exemplifies the educational philosophies of John Dewey and Maxine Greene.

Before examining the five case studies, it is helpful to gain a deeper understanding of some key elements of transformational leadership: community, mission, and vision. The ways these elements interact with each other can be seen in a profound American example: the seventeenth-century Puritans and the Massachusetts Bay Colony.

Most of us have experienced varying degrees of community, whether it is with our neighbors whom we see periodically, friends with whom we wish we could spend more time, family members who may be close or far away, and colleagues with whom we may or may not have a sense of community. These community relationships often lack a common mission or unifying vision.

The type of community related to transformational leadership and situations that may become metamorphoses requires all three elements and demands something even more profound, something that comes from deep within individuals, something that can be described as elevated or even spiritual. The seventeenth-century Puritan communities that were found in the Massachusetts Bay Colony had these characteristics. This noble group of people exhibited the fervor of first-century Christians as they left their jobs, homes, friends, and culture in order to establish God's "City upon a hill" in a faraway barren land.

SEVENTEENTH-CENTURY PURITANS AND LESSONS FOR TODAY'S EDUCATIONAL PRACTITIONERS

Model of Christian Charity

John Winthrop, leader of the Puritans en route to America from Great Britain in 1630, wrote while sailing to America on the *Arabella,*

> Wee must delight in eache other; make other's conditions our oune; rejoice together, mourne together, labour and suffer together, allwayes haueving before our eyes our commission and community in the worke, as members of the same body. . . . For wee must consider that wee shall be as a citty upon a hill. [12]

This quotation from Winthrop's *Modell of Christian Charity* captures a strong sense of community, mission, and vision as these individuals embarked on one of history's most remarkable ventures.

Frustrated that they could not purify the Church of England to meet the precepts of their plain religious beliefs, this band of approximately three hundred hearty men, women, and children decided to leave their friends, jobs, and familiar homeland to undertake an immensely dangerous voyage that would take them to a relatively unknown land. In America they hoped to realize their religious mission. It was in this new place that this mission would blossom into their vision of God's city on earth: Winthrop's "citty upon a hill."

The deep Calvinistic faith from which their mission grew emphasized that each individual in their community was elected to be among God's chosen people. These individuals were their own priests who were responsible for manifesting the written word of God as found in the Bible. Puritans joined with others who they supposed were also chosen as God's elected people to form incredibly powerful communities of believers. Such communities shaped the fundamental American character far beyond Massachusetts's shores.

One aspect of Puritan influence is found in the egalitarian nature of their religious communities. To outsiders these communities may not appear to be based on democratic principles of equality as their intensity of purpose, often appearing as rigidity, obscured the fact that among themselves each voice was considered important in shaping the community. Ministers were trained to guide members in relatively open forums that were very distinct from the hierarchy found in either the Catholic or Anglican Church.

As the elect of God each person needed to be able to read and interpret the Bible. This requirement led to the establishment of schools initially designed to educate Puritan children but later expanded to include all children who settled in the Puritan colonies. It was no accident that the first acts that would eventually grow into compulsory public education laws in the United States were the Massachusetts School Laws of 1642, 1647, and 1648. Superior education was required for Puritan ministers so that they could guide their congregations. Again, it was no accident that the first college to train these ministers was founded in 1636 in Cambridge, Massachusetts, taking its name from the man who bequeathed half of his estate and his library to the college on his death in 1638, John Harvard.

Puritan contributions to the American character went far beyond basic democratic principles of equality and recognition of the importance of education. Their awareness of purpose, for example, produced a strong work ethic. Perhaps the most profound of their contributions is seen in the passion they had for creating covenanted communities. As their population grew, these communities spread beyond New England and branded the interior of America, such as Connecticut's Western Reserve in Northern Ohio, with Puritan values and ways of associated living.[13] Common among these new settlements was their intense sense of community that was formed from both their common mission and unifying vision. It is this powerful sense of community that has drawn particular attention from historians.

Perry Miller, perhaps the most eminent historian regarding the Puritans, recognized the importance of this sense of community when he analyzed Winthrop's *Modell of Christian Charity*. He stated in *The New England Mind from Colony to Province* that "it was a 'modell' of that to which England might yet be reclaimed, and of 'charity,' which meant, not giving alms to the poor, but the knitting of individuals together as one man in order to obtain the prosperity of all."[14] Page Smith amplified the importance of community when he wrote in *As a City upon a Hill*, "The covenanted community of New England represented the most intense community experience of modern times. . . . Perhaps it was only in the primitive Christian communities of the second and third centuries or in the kibbutzim of present-day Israel that individuals have lived under such severe and awesome imperatives."[15]

Lessons for Today's Educational Practitioners

The Puritan experiment in seventeenth-century America provides many lessons regarding concepts of community, mission, and vision that can be helpful to school leaders in the twenty-first century. Understanding these concepts can be an important key for today's educational practitioners who hope to become transformational leaders who successfully combat hatred. Such leaders are able to build communities based on a unifying mission associated with social justice ideals that are dedicated to realization of a common vision.

These leaders may find the following definitions of community, mission, and vision helpful:

- Community: a group of democratically associated individuals who share a common social justice mission and are working together for a common vision.
- Mission: a set of common social justice ideals based on equity for all such as those identified in chapter 5 as lighthouse beacons that flow from our key democratic documents including the Declaration of Independence, the Constitution of the United States, Franklin Roosevelt's "Four Freedoms," and the United Nations Declaration of Human Rights.
- Vision: the social justice target—the goal, the purpose—toward which the community is moving.

School leaders are faced with daily challenges. Most of these do not rise to the level of such importance that a leader is required to make great personal sacrifices in order to accomplish the objective presented by the challenge. There are other times when—to use an expression common in Texas hold 'em poker—educational leaders are required to "go all in." This is what the Puritans did in coming to America. When educational leaders respond to particular challenges in this way, when they create communities with a common social justice mission and unifying vision, they then have the power of changing a small part of the world.

This is precisely what occurred in each of the five case studies presented in this chapter. Each of these individuals believed so strongly in their mission and the vision that grew from it that they were able to form communities of like-minded believers who worked to manifest the vision. Each of them was a transformational educational leader who did, indeed, change the world about them. Each of them combated hatred—hatred that grew from ignorance, indifference, intolerance, and prejudice—by manifesting the highest social justice ideals based on equity for all. The first case study is of Leonard Lang and the transformation of the secondary social studies curriculum in the Parma Public Schools.

TRANSFORMATIONAL EDUCATIONAL LEADERS

Changing a Curriculum to Better Understand Crucial World Issues

The American social revolution of the late 1960s was a time for deep questioning. Issues of war and peace, racial relations, poverty, and environmental concerns were among the serious topics debated by university intellectuals, writers, religious leaders, and everyday American citizens. Political, social, religious, economic, and educational institutions were confronted by fresh thinkers who challenged historic practices.

One of these thinkers was Leonard Lang, who was known as one of the outstanding educators in the Parma, Ohio, school district. Following his return from a year's study at Northwestern University in 1962 as a John Hay Fellow, he was chosen as Parma's district-wide coordinator for secondary social studies. This position meant that he was responsible for selecting, mentoring, and supervising approximately seventy-five teachers who were divided among six junior and three senior high schools. He was also responsible for the curriculum that they taught. It was in creating a community of learners to change an outmoded curriculum that he demonstrated his skills and sensitivities as a transformational leader.

At a meeting of the entire secondary social studies department in the fall of 1969 he raised a very serious concern. As an avid reader of important American magazines—such as *Saturday Review*, *Atlantic Monthly*, and *Harper's*—he was troubled by the issues that they were raising regarding the future of our species on earth. He indicated that there were four critical issues that, if not addressed in the near future, could grow into crises and result in the possible elimination of life on earth as we know it.

The four issues that he identified were:

- the possibility of nuclear war and the annihilation of entire nations;
- worldwide racial hatred that manifested itself in ongoing violence;
- overpopulation and the possibility of worldwide hunger; and
- environmental waste and damage caused by increasingly rapid consumption of finite natural resources.

Leonard's big question was: Where in the Parma grades 7 to 12 social studies curriculum were these issues addressed? The answer: Nowhere.

The Parma schools social studies curriculum in the late 1960s was typical of that found in most American public schools:

- seventh grade: general world geography
- eighth grade: U.S. history with some emphasis on specific state history
- ninth grade: civics (one semester)
- tenth grade: world history (for college-bound students)
- eleventh grade: U.S. history (required for all students)
- twelfth grade: U.S. government (one semester, required for all students)
- required elective one semester (sociology, psychology, economics) for non–college bound students

The high school curriculum leveled the required courses. This meant that advanced students were assigned to honors or advanced placement courses, challenged students were in basic classes, and most students were in regular sections of courses.

The customary pedagogy for all courses was teacher lecture based on commonly adopted textbooks. For yearlong courses these texts usually consisted of thirty-six chapters (the number of weeks in the school year), and teachers were expected to cover approximately one chapter per week. These texts were chosen from national publishers, which meant that they were written to be accepted in diverse parts of the country.

The power exerted by state school boards and departments of education in single adoption states such as Texas or California was enormous in dictating the subject matter of the books. This meant that the content was usually noncontroversial, safe, and—in one word—bland. Teacher lectures were supplemented with worksheets that were designed to prepare students for recall answers on weekly quizzes and unit tests that usually consisted of multiple choice, true/false, and fill in the blank questions. Learning seldom moved beyond the lowest levels of information gathering, and there were few analysis, synthesis, or evaluation activities in courses other than honors or advanced placement.

The history courses, for example, emphasized chronologies while ignoring the interplay between social, economic, political, geographical, and psychological forces that are important for students to develop critical understandings of historical issues and trends. Government classes stressed surface knowledge of legislative, executive, and judicial processes outlined in our national and state constitutions without exploring real political processes in action. It was no wonder that teachers often complained of students sleeping in class, even with their eyes wide open.

Leonard Lang proposed that alternatives to the traditional curriculum be explored to make courses more meaningful for students as well as addressing the serious issues that he had identified for the teachers. Teachers were generally enthusiastic but wondered if examining the traditional curriculum would involve more than simply choosing a new edition of a threadbare textbook. Lang assured them that he had commitments from the district's curriculum director and superintendent for them to develop a model secondary social studies curriculum. They were to begin with blank paper and dream as they developed an ideal. With these assurances, many teachers volunteered to be on an exploratory committee that developed a process that became a model for curriculum development that was eventually adopted by other departments in the district and elsewhere.

The model used for curriculum development began by examining expectations that social studies educators had for students on their graduation from the district. What was the basic knowledge expected of students for them to be successful in college or in their chosen career? What were the basic skills and attitudes necessary for them to become productive and self-actualizing U.S. and world citizens?

The next step was to examine the existing K–12 curriculum and determine how successful it was in achieving the expectations. This entailed teachers visiting not only different classes within their own buildings but also classes at all grade levels. For most of the teachers these visits were a first, and many eyes were opened as high school teachers visited elementary and junior high classrooms while junior high teachers visited high school and elementary classes. From these visits teachers gained district-wide perspectives and perceptions that were later shared at several district-wide meetings.

These visitations produced many ideas and questions that prompted a study of national social studies curricula. Information for this study was gathered from the National Council of Social Studies, the state department of education, and a broad range of school districts. These studies were compiled and discussed by teachers at both building level and district-wide meetings. Following the study phase, each building chose representatives to be part of a district committee whose purpose was to design a philosophy of social studies education.

In the early winter of 1970 a group of approximately thirty secondary social studies teachers and administrators met for a three-day, two-night retreat at Ohio's Punderson State Park. Their purpose, carefully articulated by Lang, was to develop a new philosophy of social studies education. He led them through an invigorating intellectual and emotional experience. Individuals dialogued, discussed, argued, and eventually agreed on a one-paragraph philosophy that encompassed not only traditional views regarding the significance of learning history and civics but also the importance of substantively addressing social justice ideals from world perspectives.

This committee also determined that survey texts, lectures, and low-level objective tests should, for the most part, be eliminated and replaced with a variety of learning materials and rich assessments. These included relevant paperback books, films, simulations, field experiences, and oral as well as written assessments of the curriculum's goals and objectives.

This new philosophy was presented to all of the secondary social studies teachers where it was, again, discussed in great detail at building-level meetings. After some additional modifications were made, it was voted on and became the social studies educational philosophy. The next step was to identify course structures that would implement the philosophy. This meant specifying grade levels, courses, goals, objectives, activities, and assessments. Based on the Punderson philosophy, it was decided to increase student choice in the required courses. The biggest change gave them an option to the year-long survey course in U.S. history and the semester course in U.S. government. This option consisted of students selecting from nineteen different courses that were offered in nine-week modules.

Examples of nine-week courses included "Black History," "Colonial America," "Crisis in Urban American Life," "Dissent and Democracy,"

"Law in American Society," "Minority Struggle," "Presidential Power," "War and Peace," and " Worlds in the Making." Changes were also made in the seventh-, eighth-, and ninth-grade offerings as well as in the world history survey course as new materials that emphasized higher-order thinking skills were introduced.

All of the district's secondary social studies courses were rewritten to reflect both the content and pedagogy of the Punderson philosophy. This was done by teams of teachers who filled rooms with various types of books and other learning materials. Lang believed that students and their teachers rather than authoritative texts from outside sources should be at the center of the educational process.

Leonard Lang's perspective of viewing teachers in this highly professional way was stimulating and encouraged teachers to respond positively to the demands made on them by the new curriculum. After extensive teacher in-service, the new curriculum went into effect in the fall of 1970. The response from both students and teachers was very positive. It was assessed at the end of the 1971 school year, and course guides were rewritten the following summer based on those assessments. This curriculum process proved to be so successful that it was adopted by several other departments not only in this district but in many surrounding ones as well.

The Parma social studies curriculum lasted for several years until it was undone by conservative curriculum forces similar to those whose voices dominated the 1983 *Nation at Risk* task force publication. These same forces are evident today in the high-stakes testing movement.

The Parma experiment had both its advocates and critics. What was clear to both was that for a period of time high school students were encouraged to be in greater control of their own learning. They responded by taking more courses in social studies than were required for graduation. Teachers were excited by the new courses, and classroom learning went from fact recall to analysis, synthesis, and evaluation of major historical, sociological, governmental, and social justice issues. Leonard Lang's question regarding where the world crisis issues of racial hatred, nuclear war, overpopulation, and destruction of the environment were found in the curriculum had been answered. It was Parma's social studies curriculum.

Leonard Lang was successful in creating a community of learners whose common mission was the education of future citizens and whose vision was making social studies education come alive by addressing serious social justice issues before they became species-threatening crises. For these reasons he truly was a transformational leader whose community developed a philosophy and built a curriculum and pedagogy based on that philosophy. In this way his transformational leadership combated ignorance, intolerance, prejudice, and the hatred that often grows from them. He sought and led others to develop a curriculum that addressed issues of social justice and equity in the richest sense. Both Leonard Lang and the community that he created grew through the curriculum development process, and a metamorphosis of the highest importance occurred for this school district's teachers and students.

The next case study is of a woman who also vitalized a community of learners through a common mission and lofty vision. The community's mission was an intense form of Catholic education that recognized social justice by doing acts of charity and providing service to others. The community's vision was to build a high school that both reflected and reinforced these values while also providing a strong academic education. The name of this transformational educational leader is Sister Rosemary Hocevar. Her school was Villa Angela Academy on Cleveland's eastern shoreline. The expression that captured the community's inspired philosophy was "Touching Tomorrow Together."

Touching Tomorrow Together

Founded in 1878 by a religious order known as the Order of Saint Ursula (OSU), Villa Angela Academy was one of the oldest Catholic schools in the Cleveland diocese. The order's all-women high school was housed in a fortress-like building that by the late 1960s was literally crumbling. The Cleveland diocese raised funds in the 1960s to build new Catholic high schools. Villa Angela was one of these. The Ursuline community who ran the school hired innovative architect Richard Fleischman to design it. At one of their initial meetings with him, the sisters learned a very important lesson. He would not begin the design process until they were able to express a commonly held educational philosophy that grew from their mission of Catholic education. Fleischman believed that if the building was to reinforce this mission, then the design needed to be a living testament to their beliefs—and it truly needed to belong to them.

The school's principal, Sister Rosemary Hocevar, clearly heard his message. The date for the proposed ground breaking was delayed for more than one year during which Sister Rosemary created a community of learners by engaging students, faculty, and alumni in numerous conversations. These were intended to challenge their beliefs and build common understandings. At the end of the year, they published a pamphlet titled "Touching Tomorrow Together" that contained their educational philosophy as well as a program and pedagogy to manifest it.

The educational program stressed Christian social justice values and high academic standards. These standards were to be achieved through an interdisciplinary curriculum that combined math with science and English with social studies. Performing/visual arts, foreign languages, business, and physical education were also prominently featured. Helping others was an expectation for all students, and during their sophomore year every young woman participated for a full year in various community service projects. The entire school program was facilitated by a close relationship between faculty and students as teachers became advisors for approximately twenty-five ninth-graders and remained with them for four years.

Once "Touching Tomorrow Together" had been adopted by the faculty, representatives of the teachers, students, and parents held regular meetings with Fleischman to design the new school. They quickly learned that every building represents a philosophy and that a school can be much more than a place to house faculty and students. Fleishman insisted that their school become one that personified their deepest beliefs. They also learned that Fleishman was both a gifted artist and a technician. Being both, his approach to architectural design was that it should embody both artistic as well as practical elements. In describing his approach to design, Fleishman wrote, "Good architecture maintains a consistent quality and image, which represent not only a network of artistic and functional spaces, but a powerful commitment to great design."[16]

The design process itself was a creative experience for members of the community as they debated different plans that would bring their philosophy to life. The experience was also an aesthetic one as they learned from Fleishman ways that shapes, colors, and materials could combine to form different environments and feelings. Creating the design helped form their community and caused them to transcend the ordinary. Sister Rosemary stated that going through this process was "the time of my life."[17] The resulting building captured their philosophy and translated it into an aesthetic, organic, living structure.

At the center of the school was a large multilevel rectangular-shaped media center that proclaimed to all that academic learning was of paramount importance. On the lower level of the media center was the library. Next to the media center, at the heart of the school, was a chapel with an altar made from a large tree taken from the grounds of the original school. By placing the chapel adjacent to the media center the design stressed that spirituality was at the core of academic pursuits.

On the main level, surrounding the media center, were semi-open academic classrooms that housed the interdisciplinary curriculum. Floating above these and flowing into the upper portions of the media center were student locker, commons, and work areas. These were next to open-space teacher carrels. Bringing students and teachers together in this manner facilitated ongoing contact and personalized each student's education. The auditorium/large group instruction room, cafeteria, gymnasium, art, and music areas were adjacent to the media center/academic core.

When the school opened in 1972, the faculty, students, and alumni were excited with the final product and recognized that theirs was a unique learning space. The school's design received praise from the community and was recognized by the Greater Cleveland Growth Association with a Certificate of Merit in 1973. The media center design received an Award of Merit in 1974 from the American Institute of Architects.

The history of this unique building took a sad turn for educators in 1988 when the Diocese of Cleveland announced that because of declining enrollments Villa Angela would be merged with Saint Joseph's, a Catholic boys high school. Today the school is known as Villa Angela-Saint Joseph's High School and occupies the former Saint Joseph's High School building on Lake Shore Boulevard in Cleveland. What was Villa Angela High School is now the Memorial Nottingham Branch of the Cleveland Public Library system.

Sister Rosemary, now retired, was an associate professor of educational administration and later an administrator at Ursuline College in Pepper Pike, Ohio. After leaving Villa Angela in 1976, she was coordinator of secondary education for the Diocese of Cleveland, where she remained until 1985 when she went to Kent State to work on her PhD in educational administration. She became director of the educational administration program at Ursuline in 1989.

Over the years Sister Rosemary has served on many boards and was president of the National Catholic Education Association's Secondary School Executive Committee from 2006 to 2009. She has made numerous national presentations on educational leadership topics and served on more than thirty North Central Association evaluation teams for both Catholic and public schools in the greater Cleveland area. Of the numerous awards that Sister Rosemary has received she is most proud of being inducted into the Villa Angela-Saint Joseph's Hall of Fame in 1995. In 2011 she received the Michael Guerra Leadership Award that is given by the National Education Association for an educator whose impact on Catholic secondary schools has a lasting impact.

Of all the outstanding work that she has done, she recalls her years at Villa Angela as the highlight of her career. Her transformational leadership institutionalized a philosophy that recognized the important social justice values of charity and service to others. These values were captured in a building that embodied those ideals. Her leadership of this educational project exemplifies the characteristics of transformational leadership as she created a community built on a common mission that manifested a lofty vision. In the early 1970s a metamorphosis happened to both her and the Villa Angela community. They did, indeed, "Touch Tomorrow Together."

The next case study is of a man who went from being a highly recognized social worker, elementary principal, and pupil personnel director in a nationally known public school system to becoming superintendent of a small, struggling suburban district. Jack Thomas's belief in the basic principle that an entire community was responsible for providing its future citizens with a quality education was unwavering. He turned a group of teachers, parents, students, and citizens into a community of advocates for children who shared his passion for public education. These believers campaigned against great odds to pass a bond issue that added badly needed facilities for a distressed school district. His transformational leadership combated indifference, self-ishness, and class distinctions based on property wealth that often leads to bitterness and hatred.

Split Community = Split Sessions

Jack Thomas became superintendent of the North Royalton school district located in the outer ring of Cleveland's suburbs in 1972. He inherited a serious problem of overcrowding as building growth had not kept pace with the increase in student population. Ohio requires local voter approval for building construction bonds as the state does not, as a general rule, provide building funds. The district had tried gaining that approval several times and failed. Faced with a difficult dilemma, the district resorted to scheduling sixth-, seventh-, and eighth-graders in the middle school to double or split sessions. This meant that the building was used from 6:00 a.m. until 6:30 p.m. Sixth-graders and half of the seventh grade attended classes from 6:00 a.m. until noon. The eighth-graders and the other half of the seventh grade attended from 12:30 until 6:30 p.m.

While this arrangement met the instructional hours required by the state, it was anything but ideal. Most of the students in the district were transported on buses, and parents complained of the great inconveniences associated with either early or late times. If both parents were working, then they also had to be concerned with extended day care issues. Teachers had no sense of a home base or professional community. They were required to make most of their instructional materials portable so that they could be bundled and taken home at the end of their session.

The biggest impact fell on the students' educational program. There was little time for any education beyond the basics, which often had to be taught during times when students would normally be at home or, perhaps, playing with their friends. Fundamental issues, such as building maintenance, strained the staff's resources to provide even rudimentary services. The matter of cafeteria service for lunches was solved simply—it was eliminated.

The inevitable outcry over split sessions from parents, students, and teachers brought them into sharp conflict with the community's old timers who did not want to pay increased taxes and see changes in their community. It was in resolving this conflict that Jack Thomas proved to be a transforma-tional leader. Ohio law prohibits the expenditure of public funds to promote bond issues or operating levies, so he formed a committee of interested parents and citizens that named itself CARE (Concerned About Royalton

Education). Their purpose was to raise funds and campaign for a new bond issue. Thomas transformed this committee into a community of advocates for children who campaigned to pass a new bond issue. Part of the campaign was to explain the proposed building plans that the committee developed with the aid of one of their members who was also a local architect.

Previous plans for an additional bond issue had called for the construction of a new high school. As these had been defeated several times, the committee suggested a very different plan. It recommended instead a major addition to the high school that included some classrooms, but also offered a scheme of shared spaces that would minimize costs and maximize benefits. These shared spaces consisted of a new media center as well as art, music, and physical education facilities.

The plan called for a reorganization of students, with the eighth grade moving from the middle school to a wing of classrooms at the high school where they would share the new media center, art rooms, gymnasium, and other common facilities. The plan seemed workable to the committee. The question was whether or not the citizens would vote for the bonds to construct the project.

Jack Thomas inspired committee members to work tirelessly in campaigning for the bond issue. Members spent many evenings, Saturdays, and Sundays going door to door to explain the crisis facing the district and the plan to resolve it. It was a cold, rainy November election day in 1974 when voters went to the polls. Many predicted that the weather would hurt the bond issue's chances. The prediction was wrong, and the issue narrowly passed. Several hundred people assembled in the high school cafeteria that evening to hear the results. After victory became clear, Jack entered the room and was greeted as a hero with a loud cheer.

He was more than a hero. He was a true leader, and a transformational one at that. He created a community and imbued it with his passion for public education. In this way he combated indifference and selfishness that can lead to rigid class distinctions and hatred. A passion for public education became the community's common mission. The mission was crystallized in a vision for new facilities that eventually not only eliminated split sessions but also led to the development of a creative middle school curriculum.

Jack Thomas left North Royalton in 1986, but he did not retire. He entered another career in which he acted as a temporary superintendent for nine different school districts while they sought permanent replacements for their top position. For these and many other reasons, today he is known as the dean of public school superintendents in Northern Ohio. Of all his accomplishments his greatest was his leadership in the watershed year of 1974 that transformed North Royalton from a struggling school district to one that is recognized among the best in the area today. This was a true metamorphosis as a community's shared mission and common vision became a reality.

The next case study is of an individual who represents in a most profound way the essential elements of transformational leadership. Alberto Hurtado was a lawyer, educator, and Chilean Jesuit who studied the educational philosophy of John Dewey. He blended Dewey's beliefs in child-centered education, democracy, and social reform with his Jesuit values of social justice to create a community whose mission was to serve society's most impoverished individuals. His vision helped create a charity for homeless Chileans named Hogar de Cristo (Christ's Home) that is recognized today as one of the most important in Latin America.

In this way Hurtado confronted the hatred and prejudice that grows from ignorance and indifference in a society of rigid classes wherein the wealthy elite are seldom in contact with the disadvantaged poor. Hurtado's transformational leadership caused a metamorphosis in Chilean society that was recognized by Pope Benedict XVI's canonization of him as a saint in 2005.

Jesuit, Educator, and Social Activist

Alberto Hurtado was born in 1901 into a relatively modest family at Viña del Mar located approximately forty-five miles from downtown Santiago. While he was still young, his father died and his mother lost the family's modest source of income from a small estate and had to live with various relatives. Hurtado worked numerous jobs in order to attend college where he became a lawyer and helped to support his family until his mother regained some of the income from her estate. It was at this time that he felt freed from family responsibilities and pursued his dream of becoming a Jesuit. [18]

He entered the Jesuit novitiate at Chillan in 1923, made his first vows two years later, and was ordained a priest in 1933. During these years of formation, he did considerable social work among the poor in various cities and continued his studies in education, languages, and the humanities. He spent the years immediately preceding his ordination studying theology in Spain until he and other Jesuits were forced to leave in 1931 because of tensions related to the impending Spanish Civil War. He completed his studies in Belgium and was ordained in Mechlen (Malines) on August 24, 1933.

Upon returning to Chile soon after his ordination, he taught religion at Saint Ignatius High School and helped train teachers at the Catholic University in Santiago. He also spent considerable time leading retreats for young men and working among the poor in the city. At the urging of the Chilean Ministry of Education, he went to the Catholic University of Louvain, Belgium, in 1934 to continue his studies in education. He completed these in 1935 and was awarded his doctoral degree in education. After spending one year traveling throughout Europe to study various educational systems, he returned to Chile in 1936. After his return he taught religion at Saint Ignatius High School and was made responsible for the spiritual direction of older students. He was also engaged in youth ministry throughout Santiago and in charge of weekly conferences of students at Catholic University.

Alberto Hurtado began writing at this time on current educational pedagogy and social reform for magazines such as *Estudios*. He also published a book in 1941, *Is Chile a Catholic Country?*, that demonstrated his strong empathy for Chile's poorer classes. This book shone a national spotlight on him as it challenged the status quo and confronted Chile's elite establishment. At this same time he became the national director and chaplain for the youth branch of an organization called Catholic Action.

Hurtado inspired these young men to become activists in bringing about reform based on Catholic social justice ideals. He became a very popular leader among the young but was criticized by conservative elements of both Chile's Catholic Church and its upper-class aristocracy. For these criticisms and other personal reasons he offered his resignation from his positions at Catholic Action. This was accepted on November 10, 1944. At approximately this same time the most important work of his life was beginning.

Christ's Home: Hogar de Cristo

On October 19, 1944, Alberto Hurtado was saying mass for a group of women who were on a retreat at the Casa del Apostolado Popular in Santiago. He stopped after reading the Gospel story of the multiplication of bread and told them that he had difficulty continuing with his planned remarks. Instead, according to a biographer of his, Katherine Gilfeather, he said,

> I have something to say to you. How can we go on with this? I didn't sleep last night and I think you would have suffered from insomnia as well had you seen what I saw. I was arriving at St. Ignatius [Hurtado's residence in Santiago] late last night when a man stopped me. He was standing there in shirtsleeves in the freezing drizzle. He was thin as a rail and shaking with fever. The lamplight was sufficient to show me that his tonsils were inflamed. He had no place to sleep and he asked me for the price of a bed in a hostel. There are hundreds of men like this in Santiago and they are all our brothers, and that is no metaphor. Each one of these men is Christ, and what have we done for them? What has the Catholic Church in Chile done for these sons of hers who walk the streets in the rain and sleep in doorways in the cold nights of winter, their bodies found frozen in the early dawn?[19]

The women were deeply moved. Some responded immediately and gave him expensive rings and broaches to start a project to help the homeless. One woman offered him land for a building while another wrote a check to cover initial construction costs. This was the birth of Hogar de Cristo or Christ's Home.

Hogar de Cristo's original purpose was both simple and profound. It was "to give a roof to the homeless beggar, food for his stomach, education and, if possible, work that would help him escape his terrible misery."[20] Only two months later, on December 21, 1944, the archbishop of Santiago blessed the cornerstone for Hogar de Cristo's initial building. Soon after the building's completion, Alberto Hurtado purchased a 1946 green Ford pickup truck that was recognized throughout Santiago as he drove it throughout the city's poorest areas in the evenings to take homeless men, women, and children to the shelter. By the early 1950s, Hogar de Cristo had expanded its mission as a shelter by adding educational and job training programs as well as providing assistance to individuals seeking employment. Its social outreach programs were popularized by a publication started by Hurtado in 1951 called *Mensaje* (Message).

ReVista, a publication of the David Rockefeller Center for Latin American Studies at Harvard University, reported that by 1951 Hogar de Cristo had housed approximately 700,000 people and had provided more than 1,800,000 food rations. It has become an important international foundation providing programs for distressed people in various countries of South America. Hogar de Cristo's programs have expanded beyond night shelters, basic education, and job training to include preschools, care for the elderly, services for those with physical and mental disabilities, assistance in providing basic housing, and extensive health care services.[21]

Alberto Hurtado died of pancreatic cancer on August 18, 1951. His body is entombed in an inspiring yet simple monument next to the original Hogar de Cristo shelter located in one of Santiago's poorest districts. Over the years there were some attempts to clear this area. One plan called for a superhighway to be built through one of the most distressed neighborhoods. These plans were rejected because of public opposition.

Millions of Chileans associate Alberto Hurtado's greatness to be his solidarity with those in distress. The simple homes of the poor fittingly add to his adjacent memorial. This solidarity and his strong sense of social justice are the essence of his life. Roots for these values are found primarily in his Catholic and Jesuit beliefs. Sources are also found in his philosophy of education, which was shaped in many important ways by the Progressive American educator John Dewey.

Alberto Hurtado's Social Justice Values

Being a member of the Society of Jesus, or a Jesuit, begins with being inspired by the life and teachings of the society's founder, Saint Ignatius of Loyola.[22] Born into a relatively noble family in Loyola, Spain, in 1491, Iñigo, as Ignatius was then known, grew to be a courtier and respected soldier. In defending the citadel at Pamplona against a French invasion in 1521, he had his right leg shattered by a cannon ball.

During his lengthy and painful recuperation at Loyola, he read books on the lives of Jesus and various saints and meditated on his own life. Following his recovery, he determined to devote his life to the service of Jesus Christ and the Catholic Church. He experienced a deep conversion while staying at the Benedictine monastery at Montserrat in 1522. His conversion deepened when he became an ascetic and spent several months in a cave near Manresa in Catalonia.

Soon after these spiritual experiences, Ignatius decided to study theology and become a priest. Dissatisfied with the rigidity of the Universities of Alcala and Salamanca in Spain, he traveled to Paris where he spent approximately seven years and eventually received his master's degree from the University of Paris. It was in Paris that he met six other men, including Francis Xavier and Peter Faber, who formed the initial Society of Jesus. All of these men were led by Ignatius through what has become known as the Spiritual Exercises that Ignatius began formulating while in Manresa.

A key to understanding Alberto Hurtado's values regarding social justice lies in understanding the importance of the Spiritual Exercises in forming a person's life. For thirty days a participant in the exercises meditates on certain aspects of the Bible with an emphasis on the life and ministry of Jesus as related in the New Testament.[23] The participant meets regularly with a spiritual adviser who guides but does not regulate the meditations.

One aspect of the exercises is that participants reflect deeply on particular experiences and scenes in Jesus's life. For example, after reading John's New Testament account of Jesus's call to two of the first disciples, the participant might picture the time of day, feel the weather, breathe in the air, and imagine the river or dry land smells, hear the sounds of children and adults talking, and then listen to the words of Jesus when he said, "What are you looking for?" Their response was, "Where do you live, Rabbi?" Jesus answered, "Come and see."[24] This scene can be imagined as a plain, powerful, and intimate dialogue. Jesus's invitation for the two to join him at his house for conversation and perhaps some tea, a glass of wine, or a beer both humanizes and spiritualizes this scene.

A Jesuit meditates regularly in this way to gain an intimacy with Jesus Christ. Jesuits also examine their actions daily to ascertain where they are or are not consistent with Christ-like values. Recognizing these types of reflection and meditation can help explain Hurtado's words to the women assembled for the retreat on October 19, 1944. When he spoke of the sick man freezing in the cold rain, he said, "Each one of these men is Christ." In Hurtado's mind these were not empty words. He believed that this was, indeed, Christ before him. This example gives greater understanding to two additional Jesuit expressions that capture part of the order's operating philosophy: "finding God in all things" and "care of the person (*cura personalis*)."[25]

"Finding God in all things" is an open-minded Jesuit concept that accepts all individuals for the sacredness of life that they represent. It helps explain the success that Jesuits have in conducting social justice activities with people of various religious beliefs in diverse parts of the world.[26] *Cura personalis* summarizes the Jesuit belief that concern for the well-being of all individuals should be a prime motivator for their actions.

From their beginnings, the Jesuits believed that their faith must be manifested in the world and not behind cloistered walls. Soon after its founding, the order conducted ministries such as providing food and care for people suffering from the effects of the plague and establishing shelters for homeless prostitutes. John O'Malley in his in-depth book *The First Jesuits* wrote, "The Jesuits' visits to hospitals and similar activities were more than 'good works' meritorious unto salvation; they were intrinsic to their pastoral self-understanding."[27]

A powerful example that demonstrates the principles of "finding God in all things" and *cura personalis* is seen in the care given to victims of the atomic bomb at Hiroshima when they sought refuge at the Jesuit residence on the outskirts of the city following the blast on August 6, 1945. Pedro Arrupe, the Superior General or leader of the Jesuits from 1965 to 1983, was at that time head of a community of thirty-five men living in the town of Nagatsuka that was located a short distance from Hiroshima. He described the community's efforts in trying to deal with the tragedy by healing, housing, and feeding many of the victims immediately following the explosion of the bomb.[28]

Arrupe captured the strands of Jesuit philosophy related to "finding God in all things" and *cura personalis* when he depicted the Jesuits' actions after being told not to enter the city because of the dangers of radiation from the bomb. Arrupe wrote,

> It is at such times that one feels most a priest, when one knows that in the city there are 50,000 bodies which, unless they are cremated, will cause a terrible plague. There were besides some 120,000 wounded to care for. In light of these facts, a priest cannot remain outside the city just to preserve his life. Of course, when one is told that in the city there is a gas that kills, one must be very determined to ignore that fact and go in. And we did. And we soon began to raise pyramids of bodies and pour fuel on them to set them afire.[29]

Even though these social justice activities are very important in defining the character of the Jesuits, the order is best known for its educational activities. Almost from its beginning the society was drawn into establishing and running schools throughout Europe at first and then throughout the world. Today there are more than 2,300 Jesuit secondary and pre-secondary schools and 80 Jesuit colleges and universities educating more than 2,500,000 students worldwide.[30] With this emphasis on education it is not unusual that

Alberto Hurtado began his ministry as a teacher. Two aspects of this ministry are unusual. First, he concentrated very heavily on the American Progressive educational philosopher John Dewey. Second, he embraced pedagogical, social, and democratic aspects of Dewey's philosophy by employing public pedagogy to turn the entire country of Chile into a person-centered classroom.

Alberto Hurtado and John Dewey

Alberto Hurtado chose John Dewey's philosophy and pedagogical theories as the topic of his doctoral dissertation that is titled "The Pedagogical System of John Dewey before the Demands of Catholic Doctrine" (El Sistema Pedagógico de John Dewey ante las Exigencias de la Doctrina Católica). Jaime Castellón, the Chilean Jesuit who was responsible for preparing the Hurtado dossier for sainthood, has studied more extensively that anyone else the writings and works of Alberto Hurtado. He indicated that Hurtado's focus on Dewey's theories was his way of breaking from the closed traditional systems that had formed him both as a Jesuit and as an educator.[31]

Castellón has said that Hurtado desired to work more extensively in public rather than private education as it was in the public schools that most of Chile's citizens were being educated. Hurtado wanted to study Dewey's progressive, cutting-edge writings as they advocated a pedagogy that focused on the learner rather than the teacher. Castellón indicated that he knows of no other Jesuit who achieved a doctorate by studying and writing about a contemporary educational and social reformer. He said that this was a brave act on Hurtado's part considering the context of Chile's conservative society in the 1930s.

Hurtado's conclusions in his 1935 dissertation regarding Dewey's philosophy and pedagogy provide insights into his later social justice actions. Not surprisingly, he found that most of Dewey's philosophical conceptions pertaining to relativism and pragmatism should be rejected as contrary to Catholic doctrine. On the other hand, Hurtado did find that Dewey's pedagogical perspectives, especially when considered in light of Dewey's views on democracy, "offer very interesting considerations on the immediate ends of education."[32] He summarized Dewey's pedagogy in fourteen main points. Three of these are particularly important in recognizing Dewey's influence on Hurtado's social activism.

The first of these concerns Dewey's views on moral education. Hurtado agreed with Dewey that there is an intimate union between intellectual and moral life and that community work should target a common purpose of social worth. Second, he concurred with Dewey that social ideals should be part of a democratic life. Third, he acknowledged agreement with Dewey regarding the relationship between the school and social activism when he wrote that "the school is an instrument of *social reform*."[33]

It is impossible to conclude that John Dewey had the dominant influence in shaping Alberto Hurtado's attitudes toward social justice and reform activism. Certainly Hurtado's Jesuit formation provided the foundation for his social justice values and the need to manifest these in the world. He is quoted as often saying,

> In order to teach it is enough to know something. But to educate one must be something. True education consists in giving oneself as a living model, an authentic lesson. This is what Jesus did.[34]

It is reasonable to conclude that Hurtado's and Dewey's views intersect regarding the important role that education plays in determining social justice values and their manifestation in a democracy. Hurtado's writings indicate that he deeply respected Dewey and that both men shared values regarding education, democracy, and social reform. Dewey's writings seem to have strengthened the connection that Hurtado made between education and social activism. In this way Dewey may be seen as an inspiration or a spark plug for Hurtado for it was after intensively studying Dewey's works that Hurtado became increasingly involved in sweeping social reform activities.[35]

Hurtado prophetically wrote in his dissertation's conclusion that "the saints, the great pedagogues, are men who have realized an idea."[36] Both Dewey and Hurtado were men who realized an idea. Dewey has been recognized as a great pedagogue; Hurtado as both a great pedagogue and a saint.

The months, weeks, and days leading up to Alberto Hurtado's canonization as a saint on October 23, 2005, found Santiago and the whole of Chile filled with great excitement. Large banners of Hurtado's portrait were hanging from buildings and street posts, vendors were selling memorabilia such as small plastic models of his 1946 green Ford pickup truck, and a special edition of *Mensaje*, the publication that he started shortly before his death, recapped his life's story and important achievements. On the eve of the canonization hundreds of students, many of them from the university that was founded in 1997 that bears his name, Universidad Alberto Hurtado, stayed up all night so as to hear Pope Benedict XVI's proclamation recognizing this newest of the Jesuit saints.[37]

Alberto Hurtado represents in a most profound way the essential elements of transformational leadership: community, mission, and vision. He created a community that began with his students and those whom he served as a priest. This community grew when his mission of social justice and service to impoverished individuals was realized in his vision of a homeless shelter that was named Hogar de Cristo or Christ's Home. He founded a magazine, *Mensaje* (Message), to popularize his social reform messages and activities.

In these ways Hurtado turned much of Chile into his classroom wherein he synthesized a person-centered pedagogy with democracy and social reform. In doing this he modeled an educational philosophy similar to that of John Dewey, whom he admired and had chosen as the topic of his doctoral dissertation.

Hurtado's actions confronted indifference and combated hatred found in a rigid class society wherein a few led comfortable lives while many were homeless, jobless, and without adequate education or health care. His profound sense of mission sought deep social justice founded on ideals of equity for all. Alberto Hurtado's transformational leadership caused a metamorphosis in Chilean society, and for this he was canonized as a saint of the Roman Catholic Church in 2005.

The final case study of a transformational leader who exemplifies the union of the key elements—community, mission, and vision—is that of Jane Golden, whose inspiration and leadership has made Philadelphia's mural arts project (Mural Arts Philadelphia) the largest public arts program in the nation.[38]

Jane Golden: Artist and Social Activist

Tuesday, November 14, 2017. It could have been just another Tuesday evening of classes for approximately seventy-five Saint Joseph's University graduate and doctoral students in the educational leadership department. Instead the department chair, Encarna Rodriguez, had arranged for a guest speaker to engage with the students for that evening's class. She was Jane Golden, founder and executive director of Mural Arts Philadelphia.

The large seminar room was alive with the usual cell phone checking and texting, chattering and laughing among classmates, and general shuffling and buzzing until Jane started to speak. Things gradually quieted down—and then the magical pin-drop moment. Jane captivated this collection of educators for more than one and a half hours as she told her story: life dreams almost derailed because of her continuous bouts with lupus, passion for social justice manifested in creating communities by building bridges in neighborhoods that defined the term "social divide," and a passionate belief in pubic pedagogy brought alive through the arts.

In short it was anything but just another Tuesday evening of classes.[39] Not an educator by training, Jane proved that she is a true educator of the highest caliber. Indeed, she is a transformational educator leading others in creating communities based on principles of social justice and equity for everyone.

In 1977 Jane Golden, a graduate who majored in fine arts and political science at Stanford, moved to the Los Angeles area wondering what she could do with a BA in art. She learned of grants sponsored by the City Wide

Mural Project and something inside her clicked. Even though the deadline had passed, she applied for a grant and with persistence eventually received one. At that time it would have been almost unbelievable that forty-one years later (2018) she would be the executive director of Mural Arts Philadelphia, which over the years has created more than 3,800 murals, making Philadelphia the "world's largest outdoor art gallery."[40]

For Philadelphia the journey began in 1984 when she was hired to be a field representative in Philadelphia's Anti-Graffiti Network. Here she was able to combine her two university majors—art and political science—to work with "kids from tough neighborhoods"[41] and get them to exchange their cans of spray paint for artists brushes as they painted murals on public buildings.

Jane's love of mural painting grew from these seeds as she realized that murals have special effects on individuals as well as communities. She wrote,

> Murals have this kind of personal impact. They engage you, stir questions, make you see things in new ways. I don't know if it is their intense color, imposing size or symbolic power, but they seem to be imbued with a mysterious energy that radiates outward, touching everyone who sees them.[42]

The Philadelphia program moved beyond graffiti prevention, and Jane began to coordinate with various groups in creating murals that would unite groups into communities, "touching everyone who sees them." Nowhere is this more powerfully demonstrated than in the Grays Ferry Peace wall.

Grays Ferry Peace Wall: Interlocking Hands

Grays Ferry is a Philadelphia neighborhood that went through a transition during the 1960s when white families began fleeing both the neighborhood and city. The riots of the early 1970s deepened a racial divide in which "you learned quickly around here where you belonged and where you didn't."[43] Lillian Ray, a black community activist from the area, and Jane Golden, an outsider white woman, shared a similar dream of creating a mural that could help bridge the Grays Ferry divide that was drawing national attention. They believed that a mural would help heal the ravaged community. Skeptics abounded when they went house to house and were greeted with slammed doors and semi-polite silence.

Then in 1997 a brawl between black and white men began a racial confrontation that eventually ended in the death of a white teen. This series of events seemed to be the catalyst that brought leaders from both sides of the divide to the realization that something needed to be done. Enter, again, Jane and Lillian. Lillian was now the head of an organization calling itself Grays Ferry United. Resistance to a mural project still existed, but this organization refused to be deterred and organized meetings to explore the idea further. Eventually, with Jane's help, several ideas for a mural symbolic of unity for all Grays Ferry people were discussed.

One design rose above the others. It was decided that interlocking hands was the most sensitive and compelling concept as it seemed to describe to those both inside and outside of the neighborhood what peace meant. Jane directed the project, which began with photographing several residents' hands. These eventually became the basis of the mural.

It is truly inspirational to see eleven hands touching one another in a pose similar to a basketball team's interlocking hands during a huddle prior to beginning the next quarter. Here we see a mix of warm skin colors; some nails semi-painted, some broken; one hand hosting rings on two fingers and one wrist exposing the cuff of a white shirt and blue coat jacket. Indeed, here is found diversity and the seeds for a sense of community captured on a large visual approximately two stories tall, a constant reminder of harmony and peace to those not only in the Grays Ferry neighborhood but those across the city. Next to the mural on a painted scroll approximately the size of a five-by-six-foot fence are painted the words "Blessed are the peacemakers: for they shall be called the children of God."[44] Amen.

One of the most unusual and powerful of the various mural projects that Jane Golden directed is one that has been made into a video titled "Concrete, Steel, and Paint."[45] This video describes the development of a project that brought together prisoners and those who had suffered from similar crimes to design and paint a mural that captured their deep emotions.

Concrete, Steel, and Paint

The site of the former Graterford State Correctional Institution is located on the outskirts of Philadelphia where in 2009 it housed approximately 3,400 prisoners. It was a maximum security facility, and many of its inmates had been convicted of the most serious crimes. Graterford was replaced in 2018 by a new $350 million facility, the SCI Phoenix Prison. It was in 2009, however, that some of the prisoners at Graterford viewed the video "Concrete, Steel, and Paint" and saw themselves as participants in a unique mural arts project.

These participants had been regularly involved in art classes offered at the prison. Some had heard of Mural Arts Philadelphia and wondered if they could be involved in designing and painting a mural as a way of helping to reconcile their serious crimes with the community. They wanted to give something back and thought that this was one way of showing remorse. A contact was made with Jane Golden, and she arranged for a meeting with them. Skeptical at first, she began to see value in the idea of bridging the sharp divide between the prison and the greater community through a mural arts project.

Opening a small crack in the prison walls might in some small way bring healing for prisoners and as well as some members of the community. Before agreeing to proceed, she insisted on one condition: the project could not include just the prisoners; it also had to include some families and individuals who were victims of crimes similar to the ones that the prisoners had committed.

This condition was more easily stated than accomplished. Relatives of victims carried deep wounds and were not certain that they wanted to meet with prisoners. Prisoners were leery of meeting individuals face to face who were severely pained by crimes similar to theirs. Despite the hesitancy, a meeting was eventually held between the two groups. It went better than many feared. There was initial contact and soon some conversations began to flow.

After several meetings the concept hit a snag over the design of the mural. It was finally resolved when the decision was made to do two murals to be positioned close to each other so as to show the similarities and differences of varied perspectives. The video, including images of the murals, is available for viewing on the Internet at https://vimeo.com/205242252.

This project is a potent testimony of the power of art to open dialogue and present new perspectives to participants. As Valerie Keller has written,

> The project challenges both sides to recognize and respect each other's essential humanity and worth—a small, but significant step toward a more healing and restorative form of justice. In telling this story, the film raises important questions about crime, justice and reconciliation—and dramatically illustrates the power of art as a catalyst to facilitate dialogue about these difficult issues.[46]

"Concrete, Steel, and Paint," both the video and the murals that it describes, are excellent examples of public pedagogy and the presence of shared values that constitute the essence of democratic life. This example is similar in some ways to the social justice ideals of public pedagogy attributed in the previous case study to Fr. Alberto Hurtado.

Public Pedagogy: John Dewey and Maxine Greene

Both of these educator/leaders exemplify theoretical perspectives of John Dewey whose views of society and democracy are summarized in this quotation: "A society which makes provision for participation in its good of all its members on equal terms and which secures flexible readjustment of its institutions through interaction of the different forms of associated life is in so far democratic."[47] Here Dewey connected the goals of democracy and the good of society with the means to achieve those, equality of all of its members. He also recognized the need for institutions to be flexible enough to address the changing needs of the society.

Dewey also believed strongly in the power that imagination through various art forms can have in transforming lives and communities.[48] One of Dewey's strongest disciples, Maxine Greene, summarized this concept of imagination through art as a way to address social justice issues best when she wrote, "I am reaching toward an idea of imagination that brings an ethical concern to the fore, a concern that, again, has to do with the community that ought to be in the making and the values that give it color and significance."[49]

Greene believed strongly in the idea that through aesthetic education individuals and communities can be awakened and go to different places together. Through her role as the Lincoln Center Institute's philosopher-in-residence, she brought together individuals from New York City and beyond to explore the transformative power that the arts can have. She wrote in *Variations on a Blue Guitar*,

> "Aesthetic education" then, is an intentional undertaking designed to nurture appreciative, reflective, cultural, participatory engagements with the arts by enabling learners to notice what is there to be noticed, and to lend works of art their lives in such a way that they can achieve them as variously meaningful. When this happens, new connections are made in experience: new patterns are formed, new vistas are opened. Persons *see* differently, resonate differently.[50]

Simply put, engagement with works of art can change individuals, and when their engagement is with others a community can be created that has the possibilities of transforming itself. This is Mural Arts Philadelphia in a nutshell. Grays Ferry and "Concrete, Steel, and Paint" exemplify hopes for such social justice transformations.

Jane Golden is within the progressive lineage of both Dewey and Greene. She epitomizes the key characteristics of a transformational educator and leader: community, mission, and vision. Her passion for the arts and their ability to address issues of social justice is manifested in a vision that has become Mural Arts Philadelphia. This same passion helped create strong communities among the artists and staff members associated with the various projects as well as the communities with which they are associated.

For these and many other accomplishments, she has received numerous awards that recognize her contributions to the community as well as to her profession. Among these are the Philadelphia Award, the Hepburn Medal from Bryn Mawr College, the Distinguished Daughter of Pennsylvania Award, and the Eisenhower Exchange Fellowship Award. Her passion for bringing arts into everyday life and turning blank walls into imaginative art works is unique. Combining this view of arts as an essential quality that separates us from other species on this planet with her strong sense of social justice distinguishes her as a transformational educator who is making a positive difference in the lives of thousands of Philadelphians.

SUMMARY

Each of the case studies presented in this chapter exemplify in a unique way the central concepts of transformational educational leadership: community, mission, and vision. Each of these educators combated hatred or confronted the elements that often lead to hatred: ignorance, indifference, or prejudice. Each of them did this by creating a sense of community with a social justice mission that enabled it to achieve a vision that grew from the common mission. They caused a metamorphosis in their particular situation that lifted the community to a higher plane.

Each of the individuals presented is an inspirational example of a trans- formational educator who became a leader for social justice and equity. Consider them again.

- Leonard Lang, deeply troubled that a district's social studies curriculum was outmoded and did not address serious issues that could lead to the demise of our species, believed so strongly in social justice ideals and the power of education that he created a community of learners that rewrote an entire secondary curriculum and made education more meaningful for students.
- Rosemary Hocevar led a community of educators, students, parents, and alumni to create a forward-looking building that incorporated an innova- tive curriculum that stimulated teachers and students to realize high aca- demic standards and Catholic social justice values.
- Jack Thomas's belief in the basic integrity of public education caused him to struggle against great odds and bring a community together in support of its children by passing a badly needed bond issue to build new facilities.
- Alberto Hurtado recognized the great disparity in social and economic classes in his Chilean homeland and created a community with a strong mission of social justice that realized a vision that became Christ's Home (Hogar de Cristo), a movement that has grown into one of the most impor- tant charitable organizations in Latin America.
- Jane Golden's mission is evident in her passion for art as a means to bridge differences between individuals as well as groups and enable them to become true communities with a strong focus on confronting social justice issues so as to nourish communities and unify disparate individuals and groups. These are transformational educators who critically examined

situations, judged them relative to the highest democratic ideals, and chose to combat intolerance, prejudice, and hatred.

These examples, as well as the others in this book, are inspiring leaders. Many of them combated ignorance and caused those around them to open their eyes and become sensitive to socially unjust situations. Some of them combated intolerance and prejudice. All of them, in one way or another, combated hatred. They are among transformational educators who are leaders for social justice and equity for all individuals.

NOTES

1. James MacGregor Burns, *Transforming Leadership* (New York: Atlantic Monthly Press, 2003), 24.

2. Ibid.

3. James MacGregor Burns elaborates on this definition of transactional leadership on page 24 in his *Transforming Leadership* when he wrote that it is the "daily stuff of politics, the pursuit of change in measured and often reluctant doses." He describes such a leader further in the same work and on the same page as follows: "The transactional leader functioned as a broker and, especially when the stakes were low, his role could be relatively minor, even automatic."

4. James MacGregor Burns distinguishes between the verbs "change" and "transform" attributing "change" to transactional leadership and "transform" to transformational leadership. He wrote on page 24 of *Transforming Leadership*: "To change is to substitute one thing for another, to give and take, to exchange places, to pass from one place to another. These are the kinds of changes I attribute to transactional leadership. But to transform something cuts much more profoundly. It is to cause a metamorphosis in form or structure, a change in the very condition or nature of a thing, a change into another substance, a radical change in outward form or inner character, as when a frog is transformed into a prince or a carriage maker into an auto factory. It is change of this breadth and depth that is fostered by transforming leadership."

5. James MacGregor Burns, *Leadership* (New York: Harper Row, 1978), 462.

6. Burns has elevated the study of democratic leadership from the publication of books and articles to sustained research through organizations such as the James MacGregor Burns Academy of Leadership based at the University of Maryland. His influence is extensive and has inspired many leadership theorists who have expanded on his work. Two of the key writers among these theorists are Bernard Bass and Kenneth Leithwood. Examples of their publications are as follows: Bass (*Leadership and Performance Beyond Expectations*, 1985; *Improving Organizational Effectiveness through Transformational Leadership*, with Bruce J. Avolio, 1994); Leithwood ("The Move toward Transformational Leadership," *Educational Leadership*, 1992; *Changing Leadership for Changing Times*, with Doris Jantzi and Rosanne Steinbach, 1999).

7. This author worked with Leonard Lang for twelve years as a teacher and department chair under his leadership in the Parma school district outside of Cleveland. This account is taken from personal experience and has been verified by his wife after Leonard's death.

8. This author knew Sr. Hocevar well from professional associations in different capacities but especially as members together on many North Central Association evaluation teams.

9. This author was an assistant superintendent to Jack Tomas for five years, having been hired by him from the position of chair of the social studies department at Normandy High School. We have remained colleagues and friends to this day.

10. This author has spent considerable time over the past fifteen years initiating and teaching in a joint master's degree program at Alberto Hurtado University in Santiago, Chile. During this time, extensive research including many visits were made to his high school and center of

his charitable foundation. There were also considerable conversations held with current Jesuits who have studied his life.

11. This author has studied the mural arts program in Philadelphia (Mural Arts Philadelphia) and has heard Jane Golden speak on several occasions at Saint Joseph's University.

12. John Winthrop, "A Modell of Christian Charity," http://history.hanover.edu/texts/winthmod.html (accessed January 7, 2018).

13. See Terrance Furin, "Change in a Covenanted Community," doctoral dissertation, Case Western Reserve University, January 1974, for a description of a covenanted community that was formed on the New England model by Connecticut settlers at Berea, Ohio, in 1836.

14. Perry Miller, *The New England Mind from Colony to Province* (Boston: Beacon Press, 1953), 25.

15. Page Smith, *As a City upon a Hill* (New York: Alfred A. Knopf, 1968), 13.

16. Richard Fleishman, *Spaces to Be Shared* (Milan: l'Arca Edizioni, 1996), front jacket flap.

17. Rosemary Hocevar e-mail to Terrance Furin, January 31, 2008.

18. General biographical information on Alberto Hurtado is found in Katherine A. Gilfeather, *Alberto Hurtado, A Man after God's Own Heart* (Santiago: Fundación Padre A. Hurtado, 1994), as well as several online sources (readily available), especially those related to his canonization in 2005.

19. Gilfeather, *Alberto Hurtado, A Man After God's Own Heart*, 36.

20. *El Mercurio*, October 20, 1944, quoted in Gilfeather, *Alberto Hurtado, A Man After God's Own Heart*, 37–38.

21. June Carolyn Erlick, "Giving and Volunteering in the Americas, From Charity to Solidarity," *ReVista*, Spring 2002, http://www.drclas.harvard.edu/revista/articles/view/9 (accessed May 29, 2007).

22. The Society of Jesus, often called the Jesuits, has flourished since its founding in 1540 with the exception of a period of time when it was suppressed (1773–1814) by Pope Clement XIII because of pressure from European monarchies. Today there are approximately 19,000 Jesuits with ministries in 112 countries.

23. There are several annotations of the thirty-day exercises. For example, one known as the 19th Annotation does not require thirty continuous days but replaces it with one hour per day of meditation for twenty-four weeks. This format includes a weekly meeting with a spiritual advisor and a weekly meeting with others who are experiencing the exercises.

24. John 1: 37–39, *Good News New Testament* (New York: American Bible Society, 1976).

25. These expressions are well known by those associated with Jesuit institutions and are often found in the written philosophies or mission statements of Jesuit schools and universities. One example is the mission statement of Saint Joseph's University in Philadelphia that describes both of these expressions in its university catalogues. For more information see Saint Joseph's University Undergraduate Programs, Course Offerings.

26. In June 2003 this author had an interesting conversation with a Bolivian Jesuit named Father Enrique who is head of a Bolivian educational organization known as Fe y Alegria. This organization runs schools for approximately 260,000 children and adults in some of Bolivia's most distressed areas. Father Enrique also leads several social justice projects in El Alto, a large suburb of La Paz. Much of the work that he does in El Alto is with the indigenous Aymara and Quechua people whose religious beliefs center on Pachamama or Mother Earth. When asked how he reconciled his Jesuit beliefs in Christianity with Pachamama, he explained that all people are God's creatures and that he felt they and their beliefs had become woven into his fabric along with his Christian beliefs.

27. John O'Malley, *The First Jesuits* (Cambridge, MA: Harvard University Press, 1993), 167.

28. Kevin Burke, ed., *Pedro Arrupe, Essential Writings* (Maryknoll, NY: Orbis Books, 2004), 39–51.

29. Ibid., 51.

30. Society of Jesus: Education Statistics, Jesedu, Rio 2017, http://jesedurio2017.educatemagis.org/en/noticias/compania-de-jesus-estadisticas-de-la-educacion/ (accessed January 8, 2018), and Jesuit Colleges and Universities Worldwide, Berkley Center, Georgetown

University, https://berkleycenter.georgetown.edu/resources/jesuit-colleges-and-universities-worldwide/list/organizations (accessed January 8, 2018).

31. The information and analyses in this and the following paragraph were gathered in a conversation between Jaime Castellón and Terrance Furin held at the Jesuit residence at Saint Ignatius in Santiago, Chile, on August 10, 2007.

32. Alberto Hurtado Cruchaga, *El Sistema Pedagógico de John Dewey ante las Exigencias de la Doctrina Católica* (Santiago: Universidad Católica Blas Cañas, 1994), 291.

33. Ibid., 296.

34. The Jesuit's Maryland Province compiled and translated into English several of Alberto Hurtado's writings concerning justice, social humanism, and reform as a prelude to his canonization. These were found in the original research for *Combating Hatred: Educators Leading the Way* at http://www.mdsj.org/hurtado. The site may not be available today, but information can be found by contacting the Maryland Province of the Jesuits at http://www.mdsj.org/.

35. Alberto Hurtado University in Santiago, Chile, was founded in 1997. It is a rich resource for materials regarding Alberto Hurtado and his social teachings. The author of this book worked extensively with leaders of this university and faculty from Saint Joseph's University from 2003 until 2016 to create a partnership between the two Jesuit universities.

36. Alberto Hurtado, *El Sistema Pedagógico de John Dewey ante las Exigencias de la Doctrina Católica*, 298.

37. Information regarding these activities was provided in a series of conversations between Fr. Fernando Verdugo, vice president at Alberto Hurtado University, and Terrance Furin following the canonization in 2005.

38. "We Believe That Art Ignites Change," *Mural Arts Philadelphia*, https://www.muralarts.org/about/ (accessed January 9, 2018).

39. This author is an affiliate professor in the doctoral program at Saint Joseph's University and was present for Jane Golden's presentation.

40. Malerie Yolen-Cohen, "Philadelphia Mural Arts: The World's Largest Outdoor Art Gallery," *Huffpost*, https://www.huffingtonpost.com/malerie-yolencohen/philadelphia-mural-arts-t_b_5092754.html (accessed January 9, 2018).

41. Jane Golden, "The Philadelphia Award," http://philadelphiaaward.org/jane-golden/ (accessed January 9, 2018).

42. Jane Golden, Robin Rice, and Monica Yant Kinney, *Philadelphia Murals and the Stories They Tell* (Philadelphia: Temple University Press, 2002), 11.

43. Kevin Spicer, lifetime resident of Grays Ferry, quoted in Golden, Rice, Kinney, *Philadelphia Murals and the Stories They Tell*, 51.

44. Ibid., 48–53.

45. Cindy Burstein and Tony Heriza, dir., "Concrete, Steel & Paint," *New Day Films*, http://www.imdb.com/title/tt1684632/ (accessed January 9, 2018).

46. Valerie Keller, "Concrete, Steel & Paint," *Vimeo*, https://vimeo.com/205242252 (accessed January 9, 2018).

47. John Dewey, *Democracy and Education* (1916; New York: Macmillan, 1944), 99.

48. See John Dewey, *Art as Experience* (New York: Berkley Publishing Group, 1934).

49. Maxine Greene, *Releasing the Imagination* (San Francisco: Jossey-Bass, 1995), 35.

50. Maxine Greene, *Variations on Blue Guitar* (New York: Teachers College Press, 2001), 6.

About the Author

Terrance L. Furin is an affiliate professor at Saint Joseph's University in Philadelphia, where he teaches in the educational leadership department's doctoral program helping to prepare transformational leaders.